The Troubled Détente

The
Troubled Détente

Albert L. Weeks

New York · New York University Press · 1976

Copyright © 1976 by New York University
Library of Congress Catalog Card Number: 75-27166
ISBN: 0-8147-9166-2

Library of Congress Cataloging in Publication Data

Weeks, Albert Loren, 1923-
The troubled détente.

Bibliography: p.
Includes index.
1. Détente.   I.   Title.
JX1393.D46W43   327'.09'046   75-27166
ISBN 0-8147-9166-2

Manufactured in the United States of America

To my dear friends, Julia Duda, and Fred, Frank and Heb

Preface

East-West relations, either in terms of cold war or of détente, have always lacked two important ingredients—outright war and truly cooperative peace.

In the deep freeze of the cold war of the 1940s and early 1950s, the big powers, who had arrayed themselves on two sides, rattled sabers and went to the brink of, but not into, direct armed conflict. At times of friendship during each of the two post-Stalin détentes, in 1963 and 1964, and 1974 and 1975, they held summits and made trade deals. They never could establish all-round, durable cooperation, however, because Moscow refused to call off its "ideological struggle" against the West or to curb its arms buildup.

Détente was nurtured from the very beginning, in the late 1960s, when a triangle of relationships formed between the United States, the People's Republic of China, and the Soviet Union. From Moscow's point of view, the rapprochement between Washington and Peking, marked by Nixon's dramatic visit to China and his meeting with the late Mao in 1972, constituted a new and serious threat to its own ambitions. Should relations between China and the United States henceforth evolve from normalization to coexistence, cooperation, and entente, Russia would be faced with the first radical rearrangement of the global balance of power, to its disadvantage, since World War II. Thus, for the Kremlin, the achievement of a détente with the United States, the fulcrum of overall détente between East and West, was a matter of desperate urgency.

Because of this, and other coolly calculated reasons, détente may remain for some time to come. But efforts to improve détente—with people-to-people grassroots relationships and encouragement of a community of interests rather than of conflict—have already run afoul of Soviet sovereign and ideological interests and concerns. For example, the "Basket Three" discussions in Vienna in 1974 and 1975 over the civil-rights provisions for the Helsinki European Security Conference that was to follow provided a frustrating demonstration of ideological incompatibility between East and West. The relatively poor relationship that the Russians have established with the West is indicated by the terminology they have adopted to refer to other nations. And it can be ordered on a scale to show the degree of friendship the Russians feel towards others, as is shown in this table:

Soviet Description *	Country
1 Sister country *(sestra strana)*	Bulgaria; Mongolian People's Republic.
2 Fraternal country *(bratskaya strana)*	14 full, participating, or "observer," members of Warsaw Pact alliance and COMECON.
3 Countries of the World Socialist System *(strany mirovoi sistemy sotsializma)*	All of the above, plus Albania, China, ** Laos, and Cambodia.
4 Countries with a Socialist orientation *(strany sotsialisticheskoi orientatsii)*	Egypt, Syria, People's Republic of Congo, Guinea, Somali, Mozambique, Angola, Libya, etc.

Soviet Description *	Country
5 Friendly countries *(druzhestvenniye strany)*	India, Afghanistan, Yemen, Finland, etc.
6 Principal capitalist powers *(glavniye kapitalisticheskiye derzhavy)*	United States, United Kingdom, West Germany, France, and Japan.
7 Main source of contemporary imperialism *(glavnii istochnik sovremennovo imperializma)*	United States.
8 Countries of deformed Socialism *(strany deformatsii sotsializma)*	China, Albania.
9 Accomplice of the imperialists, instigator of a new world war *(posobnik imperialistov, podstrekatel' novoi mirovoi voiny)*	China.

* Source: *Sotsializm i Mezhdunarodniye Otnosheniya (Socialism and International Relations),* "Nauka," Moscow, 1975; *Pravda* and *Izvestia.*
** People's Republic of China: Soviet press has recently dropped "Socialist" as a descriptive.

People in the West should not take too much heart from the fact that Moscow places its relations with China beneath all others. For one thing, the Soviets deem the cold war with China to be merely temporary. They are awaiting a change of leadership in Peking. For another, no major change in Marxism-Leninism, as interpreted by Moscow, has been made to cope with the adversary relationship between the People's Republic and Russia. In the Marxist-Leninist creed, the principal enemy remains "American capitalist imperialism." The people of the Soviet Union and the loyal members of the Soviet bloc continue to be indoctrinated this way. And until Soviet doctrines, which strongly influence the making of foreign policy in the Kremlin, are changed to show an anti-Maoist posture or to show some friendship for the "capitalist camp," détente between East and West does not seem to have a promising future.

The Russians also wish to establish détente with the West because they must trade there, and have done so. This is indicated by the fact that in 1974 their debt to the West amounted to $22.5 billion; in 1975, it jumped to $32 billion; midway into 1976, the East's debt to the West was more than two-thirds the debt of the preceding year. The largest portion of the Soviet debt to the United States stems from the massive purchases of grain made in the United States in 1975, and it is likely that the Russians will be forced to make similar purchases in the months and years ahead. Soviet bloc trade with Western Europe also continues to increase quite steadily from year to year.

It is possible that the trade will level off as the East begins to acquire the basic machines and the know-how with which to fulfill its own needs. In any case, trade is no guarantor of a future replete with peace and cooperation. After all, the Soviet Union sharply increased its trade and improved its diplomatic under-standing and cooperation with Germany between 1939 and 1941 only to descend into the fiery hell of war. (The same could be said of the trade relations that existed between Japan and the United States in the years prior to Pearl Harbor.)

But détente lives on; it could even flourish; and perhaps be improved upon. This book is dedicated to the hope that it might flourish, forming useful precedents in the process. But the discussion that follows also describes those institutions and processes which are not conducive to that growth, and which could lead to coextinction rather than to coexistence.

What lies *beyond* détente?

This is the question whose alternative answers are cause for both hope and alarm.

Contents

Introduction

The United States has entered the third century of its history with a newly elected president who has committed this country to continuing the policy of détente with the Soviet Union. Shortly before Jimmy Carter was elected, Leonid Brezhnev addressed the plenum of the Central Committee of the Communist Party in Moscow. His speech included an updating of a number of basic doctrines affecting détente that have been developed under his aegis since approximately 1969. These "Brezhnevisms" have been painstakingly analyzed by Professor Weeks and put into a clear perspective of Soviet foreign policy as it evolved under Brezhnev's predecessors, Lenin, Stalin, and Khrushchev.

The gist of the new Brezhnevist doctrine is that there can be no alternative to détente: "détente has become irreversible." Such an apparently moderate doctrine ought to be greeted enthusiastically by the United States and its allies. After all, doesn't it connote Soviet awareness of the risks in reverting to the "Cold War" with the possible outbreak of a nuclear conflict between the super-powers? To be sure, Brezhnev insisted in his speech to the Central Committee that "our policy of extensively developing relations with the United States and lessening the danger of a new world war remains unchanged." However, he warned the winner of the presidential election that the United States would have "to reckon with the actual correlation of forces in the world."

As Professor Weeks points out, Brezhnev's concept of ensuring détente in no way excludes the use of force in the "class struggle" between "Socialism" and "world imperialism." National-liberation "small wars" and extended Communist activities in capitalist countries have neither lost their relevance nor become an overly dangerous liability in the Thermonuclear Age. Rather, they have become for the Soviets increasingly relevant and applicable under today's conditions, which they characterize as "the shifting of the correlation of forces throughout the world in the Socialist favor."

Professor Weeks' analysis and conclusions have a particularly timely significance in view of Brezhnev's latest reaffirmation of his vision of détente and the challenge it poses for the Carter Administration. At the same time the new American foreign-policy advisors are coping with Brezhnev's notion of the "irreversibility of détente," that is, the impotence of the West in the face of growing Soviet military power, they would do well to heed the words of Andrei D. Sakharov, the renowned Soviet dissident and Nobel laureate. He stresses the need for a different correlation of forces, or working for disarmament while giving our "unflagging attention to human problems: to the defense of human rights, and to facilitating exchanges of people and information as the basis for international trust. This 'indivisibility of détente' must not be forgotten."

The fulfillment of Sakharov's vision, not Brezhnev's, would ensure a genuine irreversibility of a détente which otherwise will remain troubled.

—Dr. Gene Sosin
Director of Program Planning and Development
Radio Free Europe/Radio Liberty, Inc.

Glossary

Active detachment: a Communist party organization outside the Soviet Union that demonstrates a high degree of loyalty to the Soviet party line and foreign policy, as, for example, in the case of the Bulgarian, Mongolian, and East German parties.

Apparat (apparatchik): Communist party organization composed of full-time members of the party who are professional careerists either in the party or in the government, or both (*-chik,* indicating the person having these functions).

Bourgeois democracy: Western political liberalism in which civil liberties are guaranteed and protected. But, according to Communists, a limited condition of democracy in which the workers are oppressed and their freedoms hedged in by the restrictions imposed by the "monopoly-capitalist" economic order. (See Socialist democracy.)

Bourgeois pacifism (or simply pacifism): a "liberal tendency," says the Soviet *Political Dictionary,* "whose supporters are opposed to any type of war . . . [whereas] Communists have never been pacifists [since] they are opposed to plundering, unjust wars but support just, liberating wars."

Cheka: acronym for the security police organized under Lenin after the November 1917 Bolshevik *coup d'état;* from *chrez-vichainaya komissiya,* or "special commission," for combatting counterrevolution, speculation, and delinquency in office. One of the first legalizations of mass shooting of enemies of the Leninist state occurred on February 23, 1918, when the Cheka ordered the execution of all "enemy agents, counterrevolutionary agitators, speculators, organizers of uprisings," and other "counterrevolutionary elements." The successors to the Cheka were the GPU, OGPU, NKVD, MVD, and the KGB, the latter of which, since March 1954, has served as the main organization of the Soviet secret police.

Collective leadership: the principle laid down in Soviet writings in April 1953 under which no single party or government leader may possess absolute authority. According to Soviet spokesmen, the principle has been applied since Stalin's death in the form of discussion and voting within the highest policy-making organs of the party and the government.

COMECON: acronym for Council for Mutual Economic Assistance *(Sovet ekonomicheskoi vzaimopomoshchi),* consisting of the nine members of the Soviet bloc as full, voting participants together with four non-bloc Socialist countries that participate as observers. The former group consists of the Soviet Union, Bulgaria, Cuba, Czechoslovakia, East Germany, Hungary, Mongolia, Poland, and Rumania; the latter, Yugoslavia (a limited participant), and Angola, Vietnam, Laos, and North Korea as observers.

Cominform: acronym for Communist Information Bureau, the successor of the Communist International (see Comintern), formed in 1947 and disbanded in 1956. It consisted of the members of the Soviet bloc plus the two West European Communist parties of Italy and France. Its purposes included standardizing the party line in Europe according to the Soviet model, uniting the "struggle for peace" with the "struggle for Socialism," and acting as the nucleus for the crystallization of the world's Communist parties around a Russian-led center in Europe. The leading Cominform publication was the newspaper, *For a Lasting Peace, for a People's Democracy.*

Comintern: acronym for the Third Communist International established by Lenin in 1919. Through its various organs—the

Executive Committee (E.C.C.I.), Profintern (trade union international), and Sovintern (Soviet branch of the Comintern)—it served as the instrument for Soviet control and organization of the world's Communists. Among its purposes was to stir up Soviet *coup d'états* and revolutions in capitalist countries, "national-liberation struggle" in the colonial world, and to function as the "left hand" of Soviet foreign policy. From 1919 until its disbanding in 1943, the Comintern held seven congresses and innumerable conferences and other international gatherings. At the time of its disestablishment, nearly 80 Communist Parties were represented in the organization, two-thirds of whom were illegal organizations in their own countries. Until the June 1976 East Berlin conference of European Communist parties, the traditions established by the Comintern in the periods of Lenin's and Stalin's rule were said to be fully applicable under present circumstances. But even since the East Berlin conference, Soviet party statements on the "consensus document" adhered to by the 29 participants in the 1976 conference indicate Soviet reiteration of the Comintern line on "proletarian internationalism," reassertion of Soviet orthodoxy within the world's Communist movement, and tacit repudiation of "Euro-Communism," polycentrism, and other forms of non-Soviet Communist heresy.

Correlation of forces (sometimes, Worldwide correlation of class forces): the totality of "progressive" or Communist forces, headed by the Soviet Union and the Soviet bloc, said to have become more powerful in the years since launching of the Soviet Sputnik, the development of intercontinental missiles, and the Soviet bloc military buildup and modernization program since 1964. Materials issued during the Brezhnev period assert that the correlation of forces has "shifted in the Socialist favor." During the preceding, Khrushchev period (between 1956 and 1964), this correlation was said only *"to be shifting* in the Socialist favor."

Détente: relaxation of international tension, rendered in several forms in the Russian language, the most common being *razryadka mezhdunarodnoi napryazhennosti;* the French cognate is rarely used in Soviet materials. Various renderings and formulas of détente are found in Soviet writings going all the way back to Lenin. The term began to reappear with increasing frequency just before Stalin's death. The term also was used again in the mid-1960s, and at the end of the 1960s and early 1970s. A "first détente" may be identified as beginning at the very close of the Stalin period and lasting until the end of the Khrushchev era in late 1964. A "second détente" got underway in 1969 and has been in force ever since.

Dialectic: called in Soviet writings the "higher mathematics" of the revolutionary development of society, it is both a method of studying history and society as well as the actual process by which Marxist-Leninists claim that historical change takes place. Said by its practitioners to be a complex study and a complex process, the dialectic, as borrowed in part from the philosophy of Hegel, consists in a closely linked, stage-by-stage, contradiction-by-contradiction movement of history in which the rules of "thesis, antithesis and synthesis" apply. Thus, for example, capitalist society (thesis) is opposed by the proletariat and the Communist party (antithesis) which will "inevitably" progress upwards to Socialist society (synthesis), which last stage includes only the best and most lasting features of the preceding social and political order. The dialectical process in history is said to be irreversible and irrevocable. (See Histomat.) In Lenin's conceptualization of dialectic, the stress tended to be placed upon dialectic as a method of study and political action; it was a synthetic, intellectual process which itself displayed contradictions, just as society does. Few are said to be capable of understanding and applying this political "higher mathematics"; those who are said to be so capable function as top leaders of the Communist Party of the Soviet Union and are designated "theoreticians" or "strategists".

Diamat (acronym of dialectical materialism): the philosophic basis of Marxism-Leninism (see Marxism-Leninism) describing all the processes taking place in society and history, and in natural science. It is made up of a system of "laws" which apply to all aspects of reality and in which all fields—philosophy, social and natural science, and esthetics, among others—are said to be linked as well as reducible to materialism, or the physical and economic bases of reality as understood by Marxist-Leninists. According to Diamat, all "dynamic" processes in nature, society, and human thought are not only governed by irrevocable laws but also by on-going contradictions (see Dialectic). Among the principal political and philosophical enemies of Diamat, according to its practitioners, are idealism, metaphysics, religion and theology, existentialism, and, in fact, all "bourgeois" philosophies, which are either not "progressive" or are not supportive of Marxism-Leninism.

General crisis of world capitalism: a term used by the Communists in the times of Lenin and Stalin and restored to prominence today under Brezhnev, it describes the overall process by which capitalism will be destroyed or "bury itself" and give way to the new order of Socialism. The latest, and last, stage of this crisis is said to have begun in the mid- or late 1950s.

GULag archipelago (or simply GULag or Gulag): the Soviet system of labor camps containing common criminals as well as political prisoners. The word comes from the Russian acronym, GULag *(Glavnoye upravleniye lagerei)* meaning Main Administration of the Labor Camps.

Histomat (acronym of historical materialism): the study of history, as guided by Diamat, in which the economic "base" of society is regarded by Marxist-Leninists as all-determining. Histomat rejects all descriptions of history, aside from the Marxist-Leninist, as "bourgeois," whether they emphasize the biographical, ideational, accidental, or multifactoral aspects of historical phenomena.

Irreversibility: as in the "irreversibility of détente," the term is used to indicate that the second détente, as described in the writings appearing during the Brezhnev period, may be enforced and prevented from degenerating into a restored cold war or a hot war by the military, social, economic, and political force in the hands of the Soviet Union, the Socialist Camp, or the "progressive forces" throughout the world.

Just war: war fought or initiated for the purpose of advancing the cause of Socialism and Communism. Such wars in the past have included the war of defense of the "Socialist Fatherland" (the Soviet Union), between 1942 and 1945, and "national-liberation" local wars fought in Korea (between 1950 and 1953), Vietnam (1964 to 1972), Angola (in 1975 and 1976), and elsewhere.

K.G.B.: initials of the Soviet security forces, which include direction of foreign subversion, from *Komitet gosudarstvennoi bezopasnosti* (Committee for State Security), presently headed by Yuri A. Andropov, who is also a full member of the ruling Politburo. (See Cheka.)

kolkhoz: acronym of Soviet collective farm, a type of collectivistic agricultural organization in which the land is owned by the state, leased under charter to the farmers, and whose production, although partly released to enter the free market in agricultural produce, is strictly controlled by the state, as is wage and pricing policy. (See Sovkhoz.) Most other Socialist states possess a form of kolkhoz.

Local wars (limited wars, small wars): form of conflict of the type fought in Korea in the 1950s and in Vietnam in the 1960s. These wars were described in the Khrushchev period as a danger to world peace because they might escalate into world war. Local wars are described in the Brezhnev period as no longer invariably threatening to world peace, since they may not directly involve the big powers and may be fought only with conventional arms within a restricted geographical area. Brezhnev-period materials come close to equating a "legitimate" form of local war with "national-liberation struggle."

Marxism-Leninism: the official doctrine of the Communist Party of the Soviet Union and of the Soviet state; also of foreign parties and Socialist states allied with the Soviet Union. The "-Leninism" part of the doctrine consists of those contributions made by Lenin, before and after the Bolshevik seizure of power in Russia on November 7, 1917, which concern world revolution; armed violence to achieve revolutionary goals; establishment of the dictatorship of the proletariat as a long-lasting feature of Socialist states; domination of political affairs, before and after the revolution; by a "vanguard" of party leaders; infiltration of capitalist organizations by Communists and fellow-travelers; the use of the "political higher mathematics" of dialectics in order to formulate domestic and foreign policy; and other contributions.

National-liberation struggle: movements that were led or supported by Marxists or Leninists in colonial or former colonial areas aimed at establishing Socialist states more or less on the

Soviet model, which will assure a "non-capitalist road" of social, economic, and political development and the possibility of "skipping capitalism." The term is mostly but not always confined to Third World areas, but it is sometimes equated with the anticapitalist movement in developed countries. The struggle is said to involve arms, some of which originate in countries of the Socialist Commonwealth, or Soviet bloc. The word "war" is sometimes used in place of "struggle" in Communist materials.

Peaceful coexistence: called by Lenin "peaceful *cohabitation,*" and by Stalin, Khrushchev, and Brezhnev "coexistence," is a relationship between Socialist and capitalist or semi-capitalist countries in which diplomatic, commercial, and other types of normal official intercourse may occur, even to the point of cooperation in some spheres. It is a more generic term than "détente" and suggests a longer-term peaceful relationship than does the latter. Going back to Lenin, peaceful coexistence, as understood by Communist spokesmen, not only involves class struggle as an accompaniment to a policy of peaceful coexistence, but anticipates an escalation of class struggle throughout the non-Communist world during the policy's execution, which in turn is facilitated by the peace policy. Peaceful coexistence becomes increasingly appropriate in the era of thermonuclear weapons, Communist officials assert, not only because that type of war is more dangerous than all preceding types of conflict, but because public apprehension over its eventuality makes the "peace campaign" all the more imperative and politically effective. By linking peaceful coexistence with the spread of Socialism—especially, that the latter guarantees the former—the Communists inject Leninist revolutionism into their peace campaigns and slogans.

Politburo (formerly, Presidium): the name of the highest ruling organ of several Communist parties, including the Soviet Communist party, which originated the name in Lenin's time, dropped it late in the Stalin period, and restored it under Brezhnev. The number of members of a Politburo generally varies from 12 to 20.

Potesnit': to hem in or confine, as when America's activities world-wide are frustrated by the growing might of the Soviet bloc and by the shift in the correlation of forces in favor of Socialism.

Progressive forces: Communist, Communist-supported, or pro-Communist elements, groups, and organizations, found in Communist-ruled countries or in non-Communist countries. When outside the Communist bloc of nations, progressive forces may be either legal or subversive groups or individuals; they may make themselves felt through strikes, mass demonstrations, and the ballot, or by the use of violence and armed struggle. Their goal is said to be "social progress," a euphemism for the establishment of a new social, political, and economic order resembling that in the countries of the Soviet bloc.

Socialism: as understood by Marxist-Leninists, the social, political, and economic order existing throughout the Soviet bloc (unless "deformed," according to Soviet spokesmen, as in the case of Maoist China and Albania). Under Socialism, most people become employees or servants of the state and instruments for realizing the goals fixed by the ideology of Marxism-Leninism and its interpreters within the ruling organs of the single, ruling party. Unlike a full-fledged communist society, Socialist society involves inequality in salary and wage between skilled and unskilled workers and intelligentsia, differences between the various "strata" making up Socialist society, strong laws, and distribution of goods on the basis of work rather than need, as in communist society. Socialism is claimed by Marxist-Leninists to be the inevitable wave of the future for all countries of the world, based on related doctrines and "laws" of dialectical materialism and historical materialism.

Socialist democracy: said by Lenin (and reiterated by his successors) to be a higher form of democracy than exists in capitalist "bourgeois" democracies because the latter preserves the capitalist system of productive relations, ownership, and classes, among other things, while the former destroys this and sets up in its place a one-party dictatorship of the proletariat and an "all-people's state." The Socialist state's constitution, as found throughout the Communist world, customarily prefaces the civil rights section in the document with the statement that, under Socialism, all rights—freedom of speech, press, and assembly—must be expressed in the interests of Socialism and

must further the cause of "Socialist construction." State ownership of all printing facilities, for example, is alleged by
Communists to be the guarantee that the books, newspapers, or
magazines that are published actually minister to the interests
of the Socialist state and the Communist party. Further, the fact
that in elections held under Socialist democracy the single-list
candidates are elected by percentages of nearly 100 percent of
the voters is said to reflect the unanimous loyalty and support
which the Communist party wins from the electorate. One of
the principal indoctrinational tasks under Socialist democracy is
said by Communists to be the liquidation of "bourgeois
remnants" in the life and in the minds of the citizens, and
prevention of "bourgeois influences" from abroad.

Social progress: a term used throughout the Brezhnev period for
Socialism. It has apparently been adopted as an occasional
substitute for the word Socialism because of the latter's negative
connotation in some non-Communist circles.

Sovkhoz: acronym for state farm, a form of Soviet agricultural
organization whose administrative status is the village equivalent of an urban factory. Unlike its agricultural neighbor, the
kolkhoz (collective farm), the sovkhoz is a fully Socialist
economic enterprise whose employees are hired and paid by
governmental agencies and all of the produce of which (consisting mainly of industrial crops) is state property falling under the
five-year plan allotment system. Mergers of kolkhozes into
sovkhozes are not uncommon in the Soviet Union, but most of
the total arable land of the Soviet Union remains in collective
farms. Most other Socialist states possess agricultural productive units similar to the sovkhoz.

Tupik: commonly used term in Soviet media during the Vietnam
War meaning "dead end" or "blind alley," with reference to
America's predicament in the war.

Vozhd': Leader. In a ceremony in the Kremlin, October 14, 1976,
Leonid Brezhnev was designated "Vozhd' " ("Leader", carrying
the connotation of Führer or Duce.) When added to Brezhnev's
other honors (See Chapter 1), this most recent attribution could
have enormous significance for détente.

1

Brezhnev's Ideology of Détente

Marshal of the Soviet Union Leonid Ilyich Brezhnev now has more authority in his country than any other leader since Lenin and Stalin. The zenith of Brezhnev's power was marked in May 1976 by the exceptional unveiling of a Brezhnev bust in his Ukrainian hometown of Dneprodzerzhinsk. (Upon his death, the city will undoubtedly acquire his name, perhaps becoming Dneprobrezhnevsk.) This was the first time in Soviet history that a living Soviet leader had been so honored. Additions to the twentieth-century Russian Pantheon customarily are made every quarter century, so another was due by the mid-1970s.

Lenin's ascending curve of power began in 1900, with the birth of Bolshevism, and was at its peak when he died in 1924. The authority of the second leader, Stalin, started rising precipitously after 1928 and peaked in 1952 and 1953. After Stalin's death, Khrushchev appeared to be the emergent, new dictator. Just at this juncture (1964), however, the party's kingmakers jettisoned Khrushchev. But the inexorable urge in Russian history toward one-man leadership rapidly reasserted itself, and as the quarter-century mark since Stalin approached, Marshal and General Secretary Brezhnev held the power in the Kremlin. He was designated the first master theoretician and the "most outstanding statesman of our time," the "world figure on whom peace depends." Significantly, too, Brezhnev was referred to as a military strategist. These characterizations of the new Soviet dictator may sound extravagant. But they have some validity. Brezhnev *has* achieved a commanding position over the course of events in the world which is the equal of Stalin's. Moreover, the arms buildup alone that has occurred under his direct authority since Khrushchev's ouster in October 1964 has given Brezhnevist Russia the power to call many a tune in the world arena. And in matters of "theory," that is, the doctrines of Marxism-Leninism, and military strategy, Brezhnev has made several contributions of his own.

As the latest Soviet theoretician and interpreter of the creed, Brezhnev can accurately claim to have modernized the doctrines of Lenin and Stalin. He has adapted them in several respects to the conditions of the world of the 1970s. Above all, he has employed the Leninist dialectic to blend such trends and ideas as the "sharpening of the general crisis of capitalism," the Soviet approach to military parity with the United States, peaceful coexistence and détente, the "shifting of the world correlation of forces in the Socialist favor," and the "upturn in the world revolutionary process" into a single set of doctrines.

Still, most of the Marxist-Leninist essentials have been left intact by Brezhnev. Above all, militancy coupled to peacefulness has been retained. In the space of a single speech, for example, Brezhnev simultaneously commends world peace *and* armed violence, despite the consternation this may cause the Western leaders. (When Giscard had the audacity to criticize the speech to Brezhnev's face, at a Kremlin reception in October 1975, the Soviet press edited out the French President's remarks. Then, in the spring of 1976, Kissinger told the NATO foreign ministers in an historic meeting in Oslo that Soviet "ideological aggression" cannot live side-by-side with peaceful coexistence. Dissidents have added their own note of consternation.) Soviet spokesmen of Brezhnevist ideology, including the General Secretary himself, continually remind the world that the Kremlin will never change the fundamental thrust of Marxism-Leninism. A recent report by the Soviet government said that "some people demand of the

Soviet Union and its allies that they give proof of their peaceful intentions by disarming themselves ideologically. They merely stand aside watching imperialist reaction crush the movement of peoples for their freedom and social progress. It doesn't matter to these people." And as Brezhnev told the 25th Party Congress held in February and March 1976, "We will come forward wherever our conscience and our convictions may lead us . . . Détente in no way replaces, nor can it replace, the laws of class struggle . . . Détente creates favorable conditions for the broadest dissemination of the ideology of Socialism . . . the ideological battle between the two systems [capitalist and Socialist] becomes more intense."

In summary, the Soviet advocacy of "national-liberation war," and of other forms of armed violence, is merged with its "contradiction," the "offensive for peace." This has prompted a political joke in the *anekdot* circuit in Moscow. Question: "Will there be a third world war?" Answer: "No, but the 'struggle for peace' will reach such a pitch that not a single brick will be left standing."

The Leninist Roots

Few people, even in the Communist world, take the time to plumb the murky depths of the 80-million-word heritage of Vladimir Ilyich Lenin, the "first Ilyich." Known religiously as the "Lenin Word," The Leader's writings have been reprinted 11,000 times in 450 million copies and in 102 languages of the Soviet Union and neighboring countries. While ordinary people find Lenin difficult or even irritating to read, a few of the others are captivated. Fidel Castro, for example, once called Lenin's *What Is To Be Done?* the most scientific work on politics ever written (although Lenin once confided to Trotsky that the élitism expressed in this pamphlet seemed in retrospect to have been mistaken). And there are countless non-Communist radicals and terrorists of various types for whom such Lenin exegeses as those on imperialism, revolution, and revolutionary violence, and the Socialist state are instructive as well as inspirational.

Lenin was the inventor of Communist dialectics, and The Leader often spoke of the manner in which certain contradictory or "dialectical" combinations must be made. The Communist idea, he once wrote, "must be combined with the ability to make all the necessary practical compromises, to 'tack,' to make agreements, zigzags, retreats and so on in order to ... capture political power." A Communist who acts according to "Communist morality," Lenin advised, must resort to "all sorts of stratagems, maneuvers and illegal methods, to evasion and subterfuge." This may sound like unadulterated Machiavelli— using any means to reach your goals. But while Lenin confessed that he admired Machiavelli's "political realism," Bolshevik tactics and strategy involve more than a mere recap of the wiles of the Florentine author of that extraordinary "mirror of princes," *Il Principe. The Prince* does not guide the theories and policies of Lenin, and his latter-day pupils. The guide is the dialectic.

Nothing causes students of Leninism more difficulty than understanding Lenin's dialectics. In fact, it was so arcane that not even his closest collaborators, according to The Leader, understood the dialectic, not even Nikolai Bukharin, next to Lenin regarded as the most knowledgeable Marxist-Leninist in Lenin's day.

In his *Philosophical Notebooks,* written just before the 1917 March Revolution that overthrew the Tsar, Lenin described the dialectic as a tool or weapon that could be mastered only by "special minds." It was, he explained, a kind of political logic by which the "essences" of fleeting reality—social, political, and economic phenomena—could be scientifically grasped and analyzed. But the fleeting reality, he said, was not only passively studied by the special minds, but also manipulated by them. And since reality was full of contradictions—such as the "proletarian future" imbedded antagonistically in the "capitalist present," application of the dialectic to reality must also display ... contradictoriness. This would even affect speech and rhetoric. As the chief form of rhetoric, political slogans aimed at satisfying the base "instincts of the masses" should be employed in the form of "agitation," Lenin insisted, in order to hasten the approach of revolution. The slogans might contain essentially non-Communist ideas. That did not matter, as long as the effect of the words expedited the approach of revolution or Socialism. "Children"— that is, the masses—"love fairy tales," Lenin once said in describing the use of political hyperbole, rhetoric, and "agitation." Agitation, says the Soviet *Political Dictionary*, is the "technique for bringing political influence to bear over the masses by means of talks, reports, and speeches . . . newspapers, books, pamphlets, leaflets, radio, and movies. Agitation in particular is carried out on a mass scale and consists in the dissemination of a body of ideas and knowledge which is *narrower in both scope and content than is propaganda.*" (Propaganda is closer to the basic ideology than is agitation.) Speaking of agitation, Lenin told the 10th Party Congress in 1921: "Let's confess our sins. There were many such fantasy-makers in our midst. But how else can you begin the Socialist Revolution in our country without the fantasy-makers?" After the revolution as well, the forked tongue would prove necessary, said Lenin, since the "old" and the "new" still would be in tenuous coexistence with each other after the revolution. Thus, playing upon the prejudices of the old order might be required in order to gain mass support for the new order of Socialism.

Vladimir Ilyich was probably right in suspecting that few if any of his colleagues understood the actual application of the Leninist dialectic. Whenever The Leader executed one of his bold zigs or zags, he often left many comrades confused. On several occasions, just before the 1917 "October Revolution," in fact, Lenin found himself outvoted in the Central Committee or Politburo on certain key issues, a reflection of the fact that Lenin made singular use of the dialectic. The first voting on the methods and timing of the November seizure of power found Lenin in a minority. Also, Lenin was outvoted on occasion after the revolution. For example, on the matter of holding the Constituent Assembly, wherein Lenin opposed permitting this first and last large democratic, representative assembly to meet, he was overridden (the Assembly was allowed to meet for only one day and then was forcibly prorogued by the Communists). Likewise, on the matter of suing for peace with Germany, in 1917 and 1918 at Brest-Litovsk, Lenin's "contradictory" policy on compromising and coming to terms with the combatant power, Germany, would have been defeated but for the last-minute abstention of the Trotsky faction, which had opposed the concessionary "annexationist" peace that The Leader proposed. Finally, Lenin rationalized full one-man dictatorship for himself and for all local bosses down the line at every level of the party and government hierarchy. At the same time he claimed that "Soviet democracy" was the highest form of popular rule in the world. As a result, he not only alienated well-known foreign Communists such as Rosa Luxembourg; he also helped to create a formidable bloc of anti-Leninist Communists within the Russian Communist party known as the Workers' Opposition.

In foreign policy, one of Lenin's most famous dialectical blendings was combining *peaceful coexistence* together with *messianic Cominternism.* This is the legacy of the Leninist past that occupies an important place in today's Soviet foreign policy. The legacy passed through a crucial 25-year period of adaptation developed under Stalin, of course, and has reached Brezhnev in this Stalinized form. As if to symbolize the indebtedness to Stalin, a bust of Stalin, whose visage is a likeness of the late dictator as of 1952, was erected by the Brezhnev regime over the cemetery plot at the Kremlin Wall, ironically at the time détente was getting underway. (It was at this time, too, that Stalin was called *"krupnii teoretik,"* mighty theoretician, in *Pravda*'s commemorative piece on the occasion of Stalin's ninetieth birthday, December 21, 1969.)

Brezhnev's Blending of Lenin, Stalin, and Khrushchev

It has fallen to the lot of Brezhnev, and his team of ideologists, to update Leninism and Stalinism, and dialectics, in the era of rocket-borne thermonuclear weapons. Stalin was unable to modernize Lenin in this respect because he died before armaments technology had attained the lethality, global reach, and accuracy it now has. Khrushchev's six-year reign between 1958 and 1964 was too short to develop thermonuclear revolutionism and diplomacy. In any case, the ebullient and "subjectivistic" (his successors' epithet) Nikita fumbled and groped when it came to ideology. Once, for example, in the early 1960s, he admitted to a group of professors from the Academy of Sciences that the "party makes mistakes" in the realm of theory. "We depend on you scientists," he said—an heretical statement for the leader of the Communist party of the Soviet Union to make. Khrushchev gave mere lip service to a number of Leninisms—peaceful coexistence;

correlation of forces; the "three revolutionary streams"; revolutionizing the "rear" of imperialism in Asia, Africa, and Latin America; the building of Soviet military power "in the interests of peace," and so on. But Khrushchev was never able to assemble a consistent set of doctrines.

Since 1969 Leonid Brezhnev's works have been appearing. The publishing of his works again illustrates the rapidity and the degree with which this post-Khrushchev leader has attained one-man leadership. The writings of only one other top leader are currently being published in limited editions—those of Party Secretary Mikhail Suslov, Brezhnev's chief adviser in matters ideological. Of the Brezhnev works, the 1975 volume entitled, *On the Foreign Policy of the CPSU and the Soviet State—Speeches and Articles,* is the most pertinent for relations between East and West. In addition to Brezhnev's Collected Works, designated *The Lenin Course,* a number of books have appeared in the period 1972 to the present which have lent an ideological framework to détente, as the Brezhnev regime views it. Such a list must include:

V.I. Lenin and the Foreign Policy of the Socialist State, published by Kiev University Press, 1972.
Alexander Chubaryan, *V. I. Lenin and the Formation of Soviet Foreign Policy,* USSR Academy of Sciences "Science" Publishers, 1972
The International Communist, Workers' and National-Liberation Movement, published by the Higher Party School attached to the CPSU Central Committee, 1974.
Socialism and International Relations, USSR Academy of Sciences "Science" Publishers, 1975.
The Philosophical Heritage of V. I. Lenin and Problems of Contemporary War, published by the USSR Ministry of Defense, 1972
History of the Foreign Policy of the USSR, edited by Foreign Minister Andrei Gromyko and Party Secretary Boris Ponomarev, 1976.

Every line in these books, of course, was closely scrutinized by the party, and, on delicate issues, such as how to spread Communism worldwide without upsetting détente, there is no doubt that the highest officials in the party hierarchy took a direct part in the editing. The books provide a thoroughgoing insight into the Brezhnevist ideology of détente. The ideology turns out to be an amalgam of Leninism and Stalinism in which a good deal of augmentation and modernization was supplied by Brezhnevites. The ideology of détente also contains some original Brezhnevisms, which are probably destined to remain operative in Soviet policy toward the West long after Brezhnev leaves, is retired, or is made an elder statesman.

Peaceful Coexistence in Brezhnevist Ideology

The concept of peaceful coexistence dates all the way back to 1917. It was conceived by Lenin as a tactic to establish relations with the West which would involve normal diplomatic relations and commerce. With the coming of World War I and the overthrow of the Tsar in Petrograd, however, Lenin expected the "bourgeois revolution" in Russia, of March 1917, and especially his own seizure of power in November 1917 (known as the October Revolution) to touch off revolutions in Central and Western Europe. His long-standing notion of world revolution might be realized under conditions of the terrible Great War. Nevertheless, these relations would be maintained, said Lenin. On September 23, 1919, for example, Lenin made the following "dialectical combination" in merging the spread of Soviet-style revolution with business deals with capitalist states:

Everywhere the working people ... become aware of the rottenness of the bourgeois parliaments and of the necessity of a Soviet regime, the power of the toilers, the dictatorship of the proletariat, for the sake of the liberation of humanity from the yoke of capital. . . .

But,

A durable peace would be such a relief to the toilers of Russia that they would undoubtedly agree to certain concessions under reasonable terms being granted, terms which are desirable for us, too. These concessions would be one of the means of attracting into Russia the technical help of countries which are more advanced in this respect than we. These concessions would take place during the period of coexistence side-by-side of Socialist and capitalist states.

The year 1919, when the Lenin made these statements in the form of the letter, "To the American Workers," is also the time when the Third Communist International was established. The Comintern was dedicated to the forcible overthrow of capitalism wherever it existed in the world. Its first "Theses" were written personally by Lenin. Besides violent revolution, Lenin commended proletarian dictatorship as the sine qua non of truly democratic, Socialist government. He denied that such "bourgeois falsehoods" as freedom of assembly or freedom of the press had any validity in capitalist states. In place of such "pure democracy," he said, the Soviets had substituted rule by the "vanguard of the proletariat," in whose hands are concentrated the "best print shops and the biggest paper supplies" and who practice "Socialist revolutionism" rather than "bourgeois reformism." In the platform adopted by this First Congress of the Comintern appears the declaration:

Humanity, whose entire civilization now lies in ruins, is threatened with complete annihilation. There is only one force that can save it, and that is the proletariat. The old capitalist "order" no longer exists; it can no longer exist.... [The new order] must destroy the rule of capital, make war impossible, change the entire world into a single cooperative community, and make a reality of the brotherhood and freedom of the peoples.... The revolutionary epoch demands that the proletariat use those methods of struggle which concentrate its entire energy, namely the methods of mass action leading logically to direct clashes with the bourgeois state machine in open struggle. All other methods, as for example the revolutionary use of bourgeois parliaments, must be subordinated to this purpose.... The Communist International calls the entire world proletariat to this last fight, weapon against weapon, force against force.

In all of Brezhnev's books and current updatings of Lenin, little explanation is offered as to how Lenin could combine peaceful coexistence with the same capitalist world against which his Comintern had declared an "open struggle." By merely describing this contradiction as "dialectical," such authors as Chubaryan and the Higher Party School editors avoid explaining in detail the precise elements of Soviet foreign policy. Sometimes, authors who are writing in the Brezhnev period find it politic simply to delete Lenin's own renderings of the contradictoriness of his policy toward the West. For example, at the time Lenin was developing the coexistence policy, The Leader said frankly: "As soon as we are strong enough to defeat capitalism as a whole, we shall immediately take it by the scruff of the neck." Statements like these are never included in Brezhnev's updatings or historical rewrites of Lenin.

Chubaryan, an ideologist attached to the Institute of History of the Academy of Sciences, devotes dozens of pages to the historical record made by Lenin's policy of peaceful coexistence, as conceived and practiced by The Leader until his death in 1924. Lenin, he writes, worked out the basic tactics and strategy of the Soviet Republic which are still in effect today. "He defined them for the short run as well as for the future. He relied on an analysis of the objective factors obtaining in the world. He knew that Russia's involvement in the general political and economic development of the world was inevitable, along with the presence of deep inter-imperialist contradictions." As to Soviet relations with capitalist states, Chubaryan indicates how Lenin "connected support for the world revolutionary movement with the opening of normal diplomatic relations with the countries of capitalism." Lenin also saw the peace policy as a means of dividing the West: "In each case, Lenin always took account of the contradictions existing between the capitalist states, at every historical stage in which normalization expressed itself." While peaceful coexistence was an "adjunct of Socialist-capitalist relations," it was of tactical importance for Communist internationalism. Lenin, writes Chubaryan, deepened his understanding of peaceful coexistence in 1921 and 1922, when the "bases, forms, and methods of the Soviet conception of peaceful coexistence were formulated." This Leninist conception of "dialectical," consisted in the fact that "normal diplomatic relations, trade, and cultural exchange" with the capitalist world were combined with the *"other side of Lenin's conception* ... of peaceful coexistence as a special form of class struggle between Socialism and capitalism."

In reading Chubaryan, and the other books or articles discussing peaceful coexistence in the Brezhnev period, one gets the impression that nothing has changed in the Soviet conception of "peaceful" relations with the West since the time of Lenin. Likewise, the reader is supposed to think that Lenin in no way crossed his coexistence policy with calls for armed violence against the countries with whom he intended the Soviet state to coexist— or as he phrased it, "cohabit" (which is a bit cooler in its Russian connotation than "coexistence"). True, Chubaryan and others admit that peaceful coexistence and détente must be understood "dialectically," that is, as a policy of getting along with the capitalist world, especially in its application to trade, if it strengthens Socialist Russia, while at the same time giving "material support" (finances, arms, and ideological guidance) to the world revolutionary movement. But the materials also suggest that Brezhnev's conception of peaceful coexistence is a long-term policy, not a mere tactic for gaining time, and that it is in keeping with the "original Leninist formulation." However, some Kremlin spokesmen have recently admitted that Lenin's original, tactical understanding of coexistence implied that "cohabitation" with the West might only be pro tem. Accordingly, in his commemorative address on Lenin's 106th birthday anniversary, given in 1976, K. G. B. chief, Yuri Andropov, referred to the fact that Lenin had used the more provisional term "cohabitation" instead of "coexistence," the first time a Soviet leader had publicly brought attention to this fact. Andropov also asserted that there could be no thought in the early Lenin years of "excluding wars from the life of the peoples." Because at that time the "imperialist powers would not leave revolutionary Russia in peace," Lenin taught that war could only be postponed, that it was "merely a peaceful breathing spell," said Andropov. Then, this "younger-generation" Soviet leader updated the Leninist concept of peaceful coexistence by stating that, unlike its formulation in Lenin's time, it was now possible to regard the exclusion of war as a permanent feature of international life, thanks to the "wise policy" worked out by

Comrade Brezhnev, at the 24th and 25th Party Congresses of 1971 and 1976 respectively. War has become excluded, and peaceful coexistence and détente made "irreversible," he said, because of the protective "might and influence of Socialism, the continuing upsurge of the workers' movement, and the victories of national-liberation struggle by the peoples." *

The Higher Party School text provides additional insights into Brezhnev's ideology of détente. The book makes a strong assertion for the leading role played by the Russian Communist party (CPSU) in interpreting and updating Marxist-Leninist theory. The most important "international revolutionary task of the CPSU," says the book, "is the further development of the doctrines of Marxism-Leninism." On another page, the party is designated the "vanguard of the international workers' movement." This "out-standing detachment of the forces of world revolution" has worked out the proper tactics and strategy for the period of coexistence and détente. "The Soviet Union, the fraternal Socialist countries, and the whole world's Communist and workers' move-ment have always given first-rank importance to the strengthening of peace and security among the peoples. On this question, Communists take the position that under conditions of peace and peaceful coexistence between capitalist and Socialist states, the best conditions are provided for revolutionary activity; the best conditions for national-liberation struggle of the peoples; the best conditions for the widest possible influence of Socialism's success upon the struggle of the peoples of all continents." The stress laid in the Higher Party School book on the authority of the party in establishing a dialectical linkage between peace and revolution is related to Brezhnev's idea that the best guarantee of world peace is found in *Soviet* initiatives and in *Soviet* direction of Communist activities on a global basis.

Brezhnev also stresses that after 1964 substantial changes of an organizational nature have been made. These facilitate the realization of both Socialism and peace. "In recent years," says one text, "the class struggle in imperialist states has acquired a militant, offensive quality, marked by greater organization and

* For the concurrence of Andropov's partial revision of Lenin with the recent un-folding of a more moderate line in the Kremlin, see the discussion in Chapter 6, pp. 169-171.

readiness to conduct resolute activities in order to bring about basic democratic reforms in the struggle for Socialism." Despite ideological differences between Communists (as in Yugoslavia and Rumania, France, Spain, and Italy), all Communist as well as left-wing Social Democrats "must combine their activities on the national as well as international level toward the goal of achieving peace, democracy, national independence, and better living conditions for the toilers." But since the "present period" is characterized by "extreme sharpening of the ideological struggle between capitalism and Socialism," unity in Communist ranks is at a premium. "The generally-conceded vanguard of the world revolutionary movement, the CPSU" takes the lead in bringing about this desperately needed solidarity and in achieving a "single internationalist doctrine."

Sometimes, writings that were published in the Soviet bloc, give further enlightening explanations of the dialectical blend that characterizes the Brezhnevist détente ideology. Every step toward peaceful coexistence, wrote the ideologist J. Kucera in the Polish Communist party daily, *Trybuna Ludu,* on June 20, 1973, "is at the same time a giant step toward an intensification of the ideological struggle. . . . The ideological struggle is being internationalized; it has become global. As it penetrates with great force the various forms of social life, it increasingly influences the thinking of various social classes and strata." The "ideological offensive," Kucera continued, is like the offensive aspect "of military combat in which defense is conceived as subordinate to offense . . . a precondition for mounting the attack. . . . It aims at victory on a *world* scale." Some comrades, he complained, "have not yet mastered the dialectic of peaceful coexistence." They do not understand the connection between revolution and peaceful coexistence. True, he writes, "revolution cannot be exported . . . but there is no reason why we should hesitate to assist in this process. The [1969] Moscow conference of Communist and workers' parties stressed the necessity of an offensive waged by Marxism-Leninism." As long as Communists remain true to the ideology and its revolutionary goals, "we may negotiate and conclude political agreements with bourgeois governments, without prejudice to our ideological position. . . . The defense of existing Socialism and the offensive fight against imperialism, including the ideological struggle against the bourgeoisie, are the foremost duties of Socialist countries.... Fulfillment of these tasks," he concluded, "will require a closer bond between ideological work and our foreign policy, which is an instrument of the class policy of the Socialist state on a world scale."

Sometimes, too, radio broadcasts can turn up some interesting elaborations of current ideological positions, as this excerpt shows, from S. S. Vishnevsky's remarks over Radio Moscow on August 29, 1973:

International détente creates favorable opportunities for an ideological offensive by the forces of Socialism.... The struggle between the two ideologies reflects the irreconcilability of the class positions of the proletariat and the bourgeoisie, and the conflict between the two social systems.

At the 25th Party Congress in Moscow, some of the foreign delegations made candid assertions on the chances for revolution under present-day conditions of détente. Fidel Castro, for example, who had authorized the dispatch of thousands of Cubans to assist in the Communist capture of power in Angola, spoke of the "objective factors which prove that universal peace, the progress of humanity, and Socialism are all connected with one another." "No one can export revolutions," Castro continued, "but neither can anyone stop the people from bringing them about. The future as a whole belongs to Socialism and Communism." Le Duan, First Secretary of the North Vietnamese Communist party, addressed the congress and said this about revolutions under détente: "The present period is characterized by the ongoing increase in the might of the three revolutionary currents of the contemporary world—the Socialist Bloc countries. . . ; the workers' movements in capitalist countries, which are attaining unheard-of strength; and the national-liberation struggle ... before which stand even greater victories [than in Vietnam and Angola].... World revolution at present is in an extremely favorable position." Oliver Tambo, Acting President of the African National Congress of South Africa, devoted a part of his congress speech to thanking the Soviet Union for its "material" help to revolution on the African Continent: "We wish to take the opportunity to express the most profound gratitude for the timely help given by the USSR and Cuba, and the other Socialist countries . . . which assured the victory over imperialist aggression in Angola."

One of the outstanding attributes of the Brezhnevist détente ideology has been the dialectical treatment of the Stalinist notion of *"export of revolution."* On several occasions, Stalin denied that revolution could ever be exported, and that, in any case, this was not the Soviets' intention. Stalin usually made these remarks to foreign visitors from the capitalist world during interviews. They actually clashed with his more basic doctrinal exegeses, in which he openly expressed Soviet dedication to lending help, wherever or whenever, to world revolution. Under Brezhnev, the theory of "no-status-quo" and "no-freeze" has been developed. Since no one can stop the ongoing process by which "social progress" spreads worldwide, sometimes violently, sometimes nonviolently, talk of "freezing the status quo" is tantamount to promoting "counterrevolution," said Brezhnev at the 25th Party Congress in 1976. Post-World War II boundaries may be drawn and their legal status recognized by such agreements as those signed in Helsinki in 1975. But there are no permanent "boundaries" separating classes. Thus, Soviet promotion or support of "revolutionary" violence cannot be likened to inter-*state* "export"; it is inter-*class* solidarity.

Time and time again, Brezhnev spokesmen have maintained that détente extends merely to relations between states, not between classes or parties. That is, Socialist states and capitalist states can make all sorts of agreements on arms limitations, trade, ecology, or other matters, but these are actually agreements between *governments,* not between "peoples" and "classes." Another way of putting it is that governments, like laws, come and go while the class struggle remains, at least until capitalism is destroyed. Peace slogans come and go, too, until true peace is guaranteed by the single means of making the world safe for Socialism.

Correlation of Forces: A Brezhnevist Innovation

Marxism-Leninism is obsessed with revolutionary change. This change, it says, necessitates the application of force and violence to bring about revolution. In this vein, one of the most frequently quoted sayings of Marx and Engels is found in Volume 1 of Marx's *Capital:*

Force is the midwife of every old society pregnant with a new one.

And Engels once wrote:

I know of nothing more authoritarian than a revolution, and when one's will is imposed on others with bombs and bullets, as in every revolution, it seems to me an act of authority is being committed.

Lenin is more famous than the Marxist founding fathers for his emphasis upon the need to use force and violence to reach Socialist ends. For Lenin, force took the form either of civil war or of international war. Lenin once said:

As if history has ever known a big revolution that was not involved in war!

Lenin wrote this in 1919, less than two years after the much-touted Bolshevik Decree of Peace of November 1917. Finally, Lenin made one of his most extended discussions of force, war, and revolution in his pre-1917 work, "The Military Program of Proletarian Revolution," a long excerpt from which says:

Socialists, if they do not wish to cease being Socialists, cannot oppose any kind of war.... In the first place, Socialists never have and never could oppose revolutionary wars.... In the second place, civil wars are likewise wars. He who accepts class struggle cannot fail to recognize civil wars which under any classbound society represent natural, and under certain conditions, inevitable continuation of the development and aggravation of class struggle.... In the third place, Socialism, when once victorious in one country, does not exclude forthwith all wars in general. On the contrary, it presupposes them ... [Victory of Socialism in one country] must result not only in frictions, but also in direct striving of the bourgeoisie of other countries to smash the victorious proletariat of the Socialist state. . . . Only after we overthrow, completely defeat and expropriate the bourgeoisie throughout the entire world, and not simply in one country, will wars become impossible. And from a scientific point of view, it would be completely incorrect and completely unrevolutionary to by-pass or tone down the most important thing, the suppression of the resistance offered by the bourgeoisie—which is the most difficult, the most struggle-requiring [aspect] of the transition to Socialism. "Social" priests and opportunists are always ready to dream of future peaceful Socialism, but this is precisely the way they differ from revolutionary Social-Democrats. This is because they do not wish to think, to ponder the embittered class struggle and class wars which are required in order to bring about this wonderful future. Theoretically, it would be most absolutely mistaken to forget that every war is merely the continuation of politics by other means; that the present imperialist war [World War I] is a continuation of imperialist policies of two groups of great powers. . . . But the same era must also necessarily engender and feed the policy of struggle of the proletariat against the bourgeoisie, and, consequently, the possibility and the inevitability, in the first place, of wars and uprisings of the proletariat against the bourgeoisie.

In 1928, shortly after Lenin's death, the Sixth Congress of the Third International made this seemingly contradictory assertion:

Revolutionary war waged by the proletarian dictatorship is but a continuation of revolutionary peace policy "by other means."

On using force and violence, Stalin and Khrushchev followed Lenin in most respects. However, in 1956 Nikita Khrushchev, it may be recalled, ruled out the "*fatal* inevitability of war," when he and other speakers at the 20th Party Congress partially revised Lenin and Stalin in this respect. But the Khrushchev regime, like its successor under Brezhnev, never ruled out the likelihood of war, given the nature of capitalism and its inevitable offspring, imperialism. Under Brezhnev, "likelihood" and "unlikelihood" have been two poles between which the danger of war has oscillated.

Most recently, an old Leninist-Stalinist concept has been given a new interpretation by Brezhnev and his ideologues: *"correlation of forces."* Under Lenin, the term correlation of forces was applied to what Lenin called the "correlation of class forces and economic factors of the given moment for starting the Socialist revolution." Lenin thought of the term as including a whole spectrum of factors, favorable or unfavorable, leading toward, or away from, a Socialist (or Soviet) revolution within a given country. The same definition was applied during the Stalin period and the three congresses of the Comintern and the several plenums of its Executive Committee held between 1924 and 1943.

Lenin and Stalin included in their definition of the correlation of forces not only social and economic forces making for revolution, but the factor of armed violence, of actual weapons in the hands of the revolutionaries or the "workers." Lenin warned that the policy of starting foreign revolutions "undoubtedly satisfies the need of man to strive for what is beautiful, effective, and bright," but if the chances for revolution do not include the factor of effective brute force, revolution becomes mere fantasy, or "left-wing childishness."

After the 20th Congress the Kremlin ideologists began to claim that the "correlation of forces is *shifting to the Socialist advantage.*" This "shift" was explained as a global rearrangement of social and economic forces in which capitalism was *beginning* to be put on the defensive. Some spokesmen added that the capitalist "disadvantage" extended also to military power, but this was not emphasized in Khrushchev's time; Soviet military power was not all that impressive in those years. But with the military buildup and modernization program that Brezhnev began after October 1964, the concept of the correlation of forces began to take on a clearly military aspect. That is, Brezhnev made efforts to reach parity with the United States in strategic weaponry and the Warsaw Pact alliance was girded up to become a serious challenge to its NATO opponent (SALT talks and negotiations with the West to reduce military forces did not affect this).

The following quotations from the Brezhnev period illustrate the connection between détente, peaceful coexistence, and correlation of forces:

The establishment of the Socialist states and the growth of their military might have led to the emergence and development for the first time in history of a material force able to paralyze and crush imperialist aggression.

Marxism-Leninism on War and Army
(Moscow, 1972).

Of major importance for the defense of peace, popular gains, and the progressive movement of mankind was the creation by the Soviet Union of powerful nuclear weapons and rockets.

Communist of the Armed Forces
(No. 1, 1970).

The changes in the correlation of forces in favor of progress and Socialism, and to the detriment of reaction and imperialism, are the fundamental driving force which has created the conditions for the success of the peace initiatives of the Socialist countries, headed by the Soviet Union. They are also the preconditions for the further struggle to get the principles of peaceful coexistence implemented in order to proceed successfully. The favorable development of the balance of power on a global scale makes it possible to combine the perspectives of the struggle for peace, democracy, and national-liberation with the struggle for Socialism.

Zivot Strany, Prague (1976).

Brezhnev's ideology also has emphasized that military force on the Socialist side will make peaceful coexistence and détente *"irreversible."* The "irreversibility" of détente, as the Soviets understand it, contains the notion that capitalism and its adjunct, imperialism, no longer possess the "latitude" or "ability" to make their *"diktat* felt in the world arena." Brezhnev spokesmen usually point to the course and outcome of the Vietnam War to substantiate this claim. Their post-Vietnam descriptions of the capitalist position in the world amount to the assertion that the capitalist world is now "hemmed in," based on the Russian word *"potesnit'."* That is, the Socialist bloc now hems in the imperialists, preventing them either from "launching a new world war" or from "exporting counterrevolution." Export of counterrevolution is equated with interfering with the forward march of Socialism in the capitalist world and the forward march of "social progress" and "national-liberation struggle" throughout the "Third World."

Another new term introduced into the Marxist-Leninist lexicon under Brezhnev and related to the concept of the correlation of forces is the expression used above: *"social progress."* This is often used as a euphemism for "Socialism." Because, perhaps, of negative connotations attached to Socialism with a capital S, Brezhnev publicists prefer social progress. This is a term, too, which may sound attractive to left-wing Social Democrats. These include Marxist-leaning radicals who disagree with the Communists on the use of the tactics of war and violence but who nevertheless share many of the goals proclaimed in Karl Marx's *German Ideology* or Vladimir Lenin's *State and Revolution,* such as equalization of pay between employers and employees, state bureaucrats, and ordinary citizens; withering away of the state and with it, all classes, division of labor, law, political parties, and so on. "Social progress" is simply a good popular-front slogan.

Brezhnev's Military Theory

Lincoln once proposed that the ancient maxim, "might makes right," be reversed to "right makes might." However, this would be too "idealistic" for the Marxist-Leninists. To them, material quantities are the force what make the world turn around. Not that ideas do not have a certain "material force," as Lenin was fond of pointing out. But to Marx, Engels, Lenin, Stalin, Khrushchev, and Brezhnev force and violence are what count and are the indispensable means to Communist ends. That forceful, sometimes bloody, means are used to reach peaceful ends never seemed to bother the more radical Marxists. However, violence is not regarded by them as a value merely in its own right. There is little of the sense of Sorel or Nietzsche in their concept that violence refreshes because it destroys, or that it is a good psychological purgative for its users. To most Marxist-Leninists, violence, including war, may simply prove to be necessary, even in the age of thermonuclear weapons, because the "bourgeois enemy" possesses all manner of powerful weapons.

In the Brezhnev period, politico-military doctrines relating to force and violence have been developed to round out the various other ideological glosses made in the last dozen years. Together with the shift of the correlation of forces in favor of Socialism, a purely military idea has begun to assert itself, as in the following excerpt from an article which appeared in *Kommunist,* March 1972:

> Under conditions of the changed correlation of forces—in decisive measure due to the increased power of Socialism— the anti-imperialist forces have now acquired the ability to *impose upon imperialism such principles of international relations which are consistent with the interests of peace and social progress.*

The notion of "imposing upon imperialism" those norms governing international relations which favor Socialism is coupled to advocacy of the export of revolution, as explained in the following excerpt from an article in *Kommunist* written by General A. A. Yepishev, head of the Main Political Administration of the Soviet Army and Navy:

> Under contemporary conditions, the Soviet Union's opportunities have been increased still further for rendering support to the working people and the revolutionary and national-liberation movement. By restraining imperialism's encroachments against young developing countries, delivering the necessary equipment at the request of their government, and helping these countries train national cadres, the Soviet state makes an invaluable contribution to the people's struggle for freedom and independence.

Other writings published during the rule of Brezhnev make the following related points:

1. The Soviet Union has acquired the "historical initiative" in settling the "most urgent and vital issues confronting mankind today."
2. "Our army is facilitating the people's struggle for social progress."
3. The Soviet Union lends military assistance to the "vanguard of the new Africa: Algeria, Guinea, the Congo People's Republic, Somalia, Madagascar, Ethiopia," and other countries.
4. Noninterference in the affairs of other countries is qualified by the Soviets, as here (from Brezhnev's report to the 25th Party Congress and repeated often in Soviet materials since): "Respect for the sacred right of every people and every country to choose its own road of development is an inviolable principle of Leninist foreign policy. *But,* we do not conceal our views. In developing countries, as everywhere else, we stand by the side of the forces of progress, democracy, and national independence. Our relations with them are as friends and comrades-in-arms."

One of the more valuable sources of information on the Kremlin's present thinking about the use of arms to reach its aims in the thermonuclear age is the authoritative work, *Marxism-Leninism on War and Army,* published by the ideological division of the Main Political Administration of the Soviet Army and Navy. Another book with somewhat more emphasis put upon technical military matters is Marshal V. D. Sokolovsky's *Soviet Military Strategy.* The Sokolovsky book, considered by Western military specialists to be a thoroughgoing discussion of Soviet military tactics and strategy, civilian defense, and administration, is even better known as a work whose successive three editions have contained revealing editorial changes, to conform to the prevailing political trends.

The authors of *Marxism-Leninism on War and Army* maintain that "imperialism has grown more aggressive . . . and does not shrink from direct armed struggle against Socialism." This is particularly true of the "American imperialists." And the authors claim that their principal aim was to explore the "most effective ways and means of averting wars today and of creating the necessary conditions for making them impossible in the future." According to Sokolovsky, however, a variety of wars may lie ahead in the future, "limited" and/or "local wars." Such wars are usually called "small wars" since they are not global. They will probably be both limited (in the kinds of weapons that are used and the size of the powers participating in them) as well as local (in geographical extent). (The first edition of Sokolovsky's book came out in 1962 and made no admission of the feasibility of "small wars." In the first edition, it was said that local wars might well "escalate into world wars." But in the next year, the second edition implied the possibility that local wars could be fought which might not escalate into world wars. Then, in 1968, sections of Sokolovsky's book, including that on local wars, were published with changes suggesting that local wars of national liberation would be supported by the Soviets. This is a policy which now is supported by the leadership of the Soviet Union.)

War is described in both books as a "socio-political phenomenon." Wars "serve the political aims of definite classes." War is merely the continuation of politics "by other means," as the Prussian military theorist von Clausewitz said and is quoted in these books. War is bred by class differences, and by *class-state* differences. Among the latter are the differences existing between bourgeois states and Socialist-proletarian states. The two books were reiterating Lenin's statement, made in April 1917, that "we have always considered it to be absurd for the revolutionary proletariat to renounce revolutionary wars that may prove necessary in the interests of Socialism." Again, Lenin, in 1919 stated that:

> We have always said that there are wars and wars. We condemned the imperialist war [World War I], but we did not reject war in general. . . . We are living not merely in a state, but in a system of states, and the existence of the Soviet Republic side-by-side with imperialist states for a long time is unthinkable. One or the other must triumph in the end. And before that end supervenes, a series of frightful collisions between the Soviet Republic and the bourgeois states will be inevitable.

And Brezhnev, on page 682 of *On the Foreign Policy of the CPSU and the Soviet State,* the latest volume in his Collected Works:

> We are not pacifists. We are not in favor of peace at any price, nor, of course, are we for any freezing of social and economic processes which take place inside countries. . . . Peace, as we understand it, was what was given to the Vietnamese people, an historic victory in the struggle waged against imperialist aggression.

Brezhnev adds that "class peace is impossible within capitalist society"; likewise, complete "class-state peace"—eternal Socialist-capitalist coexistence—is impossible in the world. The weapons of the present day do *not* make future "just wars" unthinkable:

> The main political goals of the ruling classes assume a concentrated form in the political aims stated in the course of the war. . . . In just wars, the people rally and give all their powers to gain victory over the imperialist aggressors. . . . All the above will apply to an even greater extent to nuclear war, should it ever be allowed to come about. . . . Nuclear war is a complex and manysided process, which, in addition to the operation of the armed forces, will involve economic, diplomatic, and ideological forms of struggle.

Fear over the outbreak of nuclear war, Brezhnev continues, has caused some errant thinkers (in the "pacifist and idealist camp") to separate violence per se from the political aims of a future war. War cannot be reduced to "armed struggle alone," in the way war is conceived. "This fetishism of armed violence and its isolation from politics has assumed a new 'nuclear' form in contemporary conditions [leading to the conclusion that] the connection between nuclear missile war and politics has been disrupted." Such an argument is "untenable and onesided," because people become so blinded by the terror of the weapons that they forget the Marxist-Leninist doctrine that war is merely the continuation of politics by other means, and that it is the "class purposes" of a given war or any war, small or nuclear, which is uppermost. "Armed struggle with the use of nuclear missiles will ultimately be subordinated to the interests of a definite policy and will become a means of attaining definite political aims."

Very recently, this Soviet view of "just" nuclear war has been vehemently challenged in the Communist press of Yugoslavia.* The Belgrade daily, *Borba*, on May 14, 1976 disputed Brezhnev's position on nuclear war in an article by the East German Minister of Defense and Politburo member, General Heinz Hoffmann. According to this Warsaw Pact general, certain "progressive forces in the international peace movement" make the *erroneous* assertion that a "rocket-nuclear war no longer represents a continuation of the policy of class struggle but merely the nuclear destruction of the world." Under the headline "Anachronistic Ideas," the *Borba* military-political columnist, Dimitrije Seserinac, made these comments on the views of General Hoffmann:

> To criticize the "progressive forces of the international peace movement" for having been against war and armed conflicts as methods of resolving social contradictions is a perversion of reality.... To believe that correlation between forces of progress and those of reaction changes only in terms of the numbers of nuclear bombs, nuclear submarines, aircraft carriers, or modern tanks and aircraft amounts to a conscious neglect of fact well known all over the world.
>
> Nobody wishes to or can negate the significant part played by the USSR and the other Socialist countries, as well as the armed forces, in the general movement of the correlation between the forces of progress and the forces of reaction. But their role should not be to destroy the imperialist and reactionary forces in a "general, just nuclear war" in order to make it possible for all the progressive forces in the world to seize power from hands of the exploiters.

Gradually, during the time Brezhnev has been in power, the Soviets have gone much farther than conceding that local wars are inevitable and desirable; they now say that they believe a third world war is entirely possible, and, under certain circumstances,

---

* For a second Yugoslav press attack on the G.D.R. Minister of Defense, also written by Seserinac, see below, pp. 160-162.

desirable. The Socialist side, in such a war, would emerge victorious, and capitalism and imperialism would be doomed.* Accordingly, the present head of the Main Political Administration of the Soviet Army and Navy, General A. A. Yepishev, who is believed to be a close political ally of the General Secretary and Marshal Brezhnev, wrote in the Russian Communist party journal *Kommunist* in the spring of 1969:

> A third world war, if imperialism should start one, would be the decisive class conflict between the two antagonistic world systems. From the side of the imperialist states, this war would be the continuation of the criminal, reactionary, and aggressive policies of imperialism. But from the side of the Soviet Union and the countries of the Socialist Commonwealth, this war would be the continuation of the revolutionary policies of freedom and independence of the Socialist state, a guarantee of the construction of Socialism and communism, and a legal and justified counteraction to aggression.

Some Soviet statements in the 1970s contain the expression, "firm rebuff to imperialism," in what sounds like a reference to World War III, or at least to local war. Marshal A. A. Grechko made the statement, when he was Minister of Defense, that:

> In the implementation of [Soviet] foreign policy, a firm rebuff to imperialism and support for the revolutionary and liberation movements are inevitably combined with the Leninist course of peaceful coexistence among states with differing social systems.

The Marshal, again, to the 24th Party Congress in 1971 said

> We can state boldly that the Soviet Army is an army of proletarian internationalism rendering aid to all those who are struggling against imperialism, and for freedom and Socialism.

* See Chapter 6, pp. 158-161, for a discussion of the more recent Soviet view on World War III.

Fleet Admiral S. G. Gorshkov, whose rank is the equivalent to Marshal, wrote in *Morskoi Sbornik* in 1972 that the duty of the Soviet Navy is to "demonstrate economic and military might beyond the state's borders" and to "protect the interests of the country beyond its borders"—a clear indication of Soviet readiness not to flinch at the prospects of farflung local or even general wars in the thermonuclear era.

Finally, Milovidov and Kozlov, in *The Philosophical Heritage of V. I. Lenin and Problems of Contemporary War* speak of the "expansion" and "intensification" of the "international tasks of the Soviet armed forces," of their involvement in revolutionary events, the expanding "social and political role" to be performed by them "in the present era." All of this politico-military revolutionariness is a product of the Brezhnev era. It constitutes an important revision to the ideology of détente which is not very reassuring to people abroad who hope for something more than a cold peace between East and West and for defusing the ideological struggle.

The Political Use of the Ultimate Weapons

Soviet politico-military ideology has become more reckless as Soviet military power has approached parity with the United States. The emphasis on ideology combined with a military buildup has been a special and salient feature of Brezhnev's détente. Some background is necessary to see how this development evolved.

From the first appearance of atomic bombs in 1945, the Soviets began to speak of the "atomic diplomacy" as practiced by the "imperialists." Sometimes they ridiculed the efficacy of using atom bombs like political counters. But it was also clear, after World War II, Stalin was bent upon developing atomic weapons for Russia as soon as possible. Khrushchev mentions in his memoirs about Stalin's great interest in developing these weapons which looked to him like major pieces on the international diplomatic chess board. And during Khrushchev's own rule, "big-bang" diplomacy was established as the reaction to what the Soviets called the Western policy of "position of strength." The

Soviet leader seemed to be committed to a more restrained policy of *limited* exploitation of the thermonuclear standoff—that is, the use of threats and bluff to force through certain Soviet moves abroad. Khrushchev always reasoned that the other half of the bipolar standoff would fear to resort to ultimate weapons to counter his moves. After all, in Korea, the other side (the UN forces led by the United States) had held back from the use of strategic bombers armed with atomic bombs to destroy the privileged sanctuaries of Russia and China; the Allies could be trusted to show similar restraint in future.

But Khrushchev's critics felt that he did not exploit the nuclear standoff as much as he might have, nor did he improve Soviet weapons systems as much as they thought he should. Khrushchev evidently expected that the United States and its allies would not increase their military strength if they perceived that the Russians were not; his critics felt that he had been naïve. In fact, the United States began to take up the policy of "flexible response" and to develop its military forces in order to cope with various forms of aggression short of full-scale thermonuclear world war, in addition to maintaining its nuclear deterrence.

Future Wars

After Khrushchev's fall, the Russians immediately switched to the policy of developing their own forces to cope with "limited aggression," as well as global cataclysm, just as the United States had. Thus, within two months after Khrushchev had been overthrown, General Sergei M. Shtemenko declared that a combination of ground, naval, and air forces would assure "full victory" in any future war.* What the Soviets needed, he wrote, was a broader-based military establishment than the country possessed at that time. This recommendation was coupled to another future contingency, said Shtemenko: the long war, as

* Shtemenko, in the Khrushchev years, had once ridiculed the designation of ICBMs as the "queen of battle." Under Brezhnev, Shtemenko's star ascended dramatically as he was appointed Chief of the General Staff of the Warsaw Pact armed forces in 1968, the same year that he played the key role in the military invasion and occupation of Czechoslovakia.

opposed to the short one contemplated by many of the Khrushchev military spokesmen. The future war might very well be a long conflict involving many stages, many types of weapons, civilian defense, and ground forces. This approach was also explained in articles written by military writers and in books by officers whose positions of authority were increased after October 1964 such as Marshal A. A. Grechko, writing in *On Guard Over the Peace and the Building of Communism* (1971); Marshal I. I. Yakubovsky, *Fighting Cooperation* (1971); General A. A. Yepishev, *Communists of the Army and Navy* (1971); Colonel V. Ye. Savkin, *The Basic Principles of Operational Art and Tactics* (1972); Grechko, *The Armed Forces of the Soviet State* (1974); Yepishev, *The Ideological Struggle on Military Problems* (1974). An important, additional spokesman for the new view after Khrushchev's ouster was Marshal M. V. Zakharov, the Chief of Staff of the Soviet Union at that time, who acquired his post as the result of an air accident at the Belgrade, Yugoslavia, airport (just days after the Kremlin coup) in which the Khrushchev Chief of Staff, Marshal Sergei S. Biryuzov, was killed.

Defense Minister Marshal Rodion Ya. Malinovsky made his significant address atop the Lenin Mausoleum on November 7, 1964, and presented the new military look. It finally assumed in the coming months and years the following shape:

- Tensions and the danger of a new war have increased.
- The capitalist imperialists can be counted on to launch local wars which need not necessarily escalate into big wars, and which, if joined in by any Communist powers opposing the imperialists, would be just (legitimate) national-liberation wars.
- Should a worldwide conflict break out, and whether or not the surprise attack or sneak attack was used at the beginning, the war would not be a short one, although the opening phase would prove to be crucial; the long war would pass through many phases and involve many types of weapons.
- Less than Soviet Union parity in ICBMs on the Soviet side was an unsafe strategy; the Soviet Union must work

toward parity and even superiority, in this and in other strategic respects, over the imperialists.

• A Third World War is by no means unlikely; moreover, it could be won by the Socialist side, should the imperialists be so unwise as to initiate it; such a war would spell the end of capitalism.

Important personnel changes were made in the highest echelons of both civilian and military commands to conform to the changes in strategy listed above. Besides the Minister of Defense, Marshal A. A. Grechko, appointed after Marshal Malinovsky's death in 1967, three new First Deputy Ministers were appointed. General S. L. Sokolov and Marshal I. I. Yakubovsky were promoted in 1967 and Marshal M. V. Zakharov, in November 1964. Four new Deputy Ministers were appointed. General P. F. Batitsky, was appointed in 1966, General I. G. Pavlovsky in 1967, General S. S. Maryakhin in 1968, and Marshal P. S. Kutakhov in 1969. In most cases, these appointees, usually in their mid- to late fifties, were believed by Western specialists to lean toward more active use or the threat of the use of arms to realize Soviet ideological goals worldwide than their predecessors had. The Russians applied the concept of the "use of arms" indirectly, as in Vietnam, the Middle East, and Angola, or when they shipped arms to their followers in the world outside of the Soviet Union.

The Professional Military Enter Politics

In the late 1960s, the professional military men became concerned with the use of the military buildup to influence politics and foreign policy. Their concern is expressed in a book by Major General A. S. Milovidov and Colonel V. G. Kozlov entitled *The Philosophical Heritage of V. I. Lenin and Problems of Contemporary War*. The language is frank:

Lenin focused attention on the interaction between offense and defense and pointed out the specific features of both types of combat operations.... The *offensive character* of Soviet strategy is explained in large degree by the *very nature of organization of the revolutionary proletariat and its army, by the active nature of Communist ideology,* with which the political and military leaders of the proletarian masses are armed. Frunze stated in connection with this that the features of maneuverability, resoluteness and aggressiveness which are inherent in the Red Army "were connected not only with the objective conditions of military operations, a fact which nobody denies, but also with the fact that *at the head of the Red Army stood elements permeated with the vigorous, aggressive ideology* of the worker class. . . . Employment of nuclear weapons in the defensive operation and engagement increases the stability of defense and enables the defending force to mount heavy strikes against the opposing enemy force *even before the attack begins. . . .*" Lenin demonstrated enormous importance to gaining and holding the strategic initiative. He considered possession of strategic initiative and suppression of enemy freedom of action to be one of the most important conditions for success in combat. Lenin demonstrated that the initiative character of armed combat by the proletariat is objectively conditioned by the fact that it is a class which is conducting *an historic offensive against the old system.*

To be noted is the reference to the "active" or "aggressive" nature of Marxism-Leninism, that it is the doctrine of the "class which is conducting an historic offensive against the old system." It is acceptable in this doctrine to begin a nuclear attack "even before the attack begins" from the other side. It is not clear whether nuclear weapons are to be used tactically or strategically.

Other Soviet writings in recent years have stressed the use of the "factor of surprise" in the very opening phase of a third world war. However, there also has been an indication that the Soviets think that the "shift in the correlation of forces in favor of Socialism," in the military as well as nonmilitary sense, has made it possible to preclude a nuclear war altogether. Sometimes the word used by the Soviets in this context is "cut off," "to cut off the launching of a new war." Sometimes the word used is "preempt," "break up," or simply "destroy." Whatever term is employed, the notion that is communicated is that Soviet military policy and strategy are presently geared to preventing imperialist initiatives by force in launching either a local war or a general war. It is further indicated that a military buildup on the Soviet side "limits" or "confines" the freedom of action of the other side in the present period of "imperialist preparations for a new world war," a much-used phrase in recent Soviet military writings. Diplomatic strategy seems geared to the same policy.

On Isolation of the United States

In military strategy, as presently disclosed in Soviet military writings, the isolation of the United States may be achieved in several ways. The Soviets have aimed at isolating America from its European allies. To accomplish this, Communist and pro-Communist forces in West European capitalist countries once used the slogan, "Yankee Go Home!" and "Europe-for-Europeans" for the same purpose. Stress is put on the fact that America is geographically isolated, to begin with; and that she is the main initiator of cold war and "counterrevolutionary" hot wars, as in Korea and Vietnam. The Russians also have concentrated on isolating the United States from the capitalist "rear" in Asia, Africa, and Latin America. If most of the whole Third World complex of nations, which number about four-fifths of all the nations of the world, can either be neutralized or, even better, attracted to the Socialist camp, America's isolation is enhanced. If the Soviet strategy were successful, the day could arrive when the United States would become the isolated enemy. NATO and other military blocs, supported mainly by the United States, would have crumbled. And Western states would undergo internal changes, including Communist takeovers, by which their separation from alliances with the United States could be expedited. Either through the use of a nuclear-missile offensive, or the threat of the use of the offensive, any "counterrevolutionary" action by the United States would be precluded, and capitalism encircled and liquidated.

If the scenario described above does indeed underlie present Soviet strategy, as it appears to at present, the prime test for its execution will be actual Soviet application of the concept of "correlation of forces in favor of Socialism." Both civilian and military writers suggest that the change in this correlation or balance (or imbalance, in the Soviet bloc's favor) is already having a telling effect worldwide. No longer, it is maintained in Soviet writings, can the United States' *diktat* be carried out all over the globe. The "inevitable process" by which "social progress" is spreading throughout the world can no longer be frustrated by any move on the part of the United States.

In reality, another confrontation between the East and West, such as that which was made during the Cuban missile crisis, will be required to test Brezhnev's new policy. It would, of course, provide a most serious challenge to détente and peaceful coexistence and to the nerve of the Western nations as well.

2

The Leninist Legacy of "Peaceful Coexistence" and Cominternism

Lenin's ideas form the basis of the theory and practice of Soviet foreign policy, especially that related to peaceful coexistence as a form of class struggle. And during the first years that Lenin pursued his policy, he accomplished four major achievements towards establishing peaceful coexistence. These were the Decree of Peace, of 1917; the Brest-Litovsk Treaty, of 1918; the founding of the Third Communist International, in 1919; and the Genoa Conference, in 1922.

The Decree of Peace

"Peace, land and bread" was the famous Lenin slogan on the eve of the Bolshevik seizure of power in Russia in November 1917. Not by accident, the Bolsheviks led off their slogan with the word "peace," the cause "most dear to the hearts of the toilers." And with the peace slogan, Lenin displayed that double meaning that characterized so many of his statements. On the one hand, he restated his "principled" philosophical position in favor of peace, and, on the other hand, he exploited the slogan for political effect, for the purposes of agitation.

Alexander Chubaryan's authoritative book, *V. I. Lenin and the Formation of Soviet Foreign Policy* (1972), discusses the "dialectical" way in which Lenin understood the concepts and the true nature of war and peace. The Soviet author states that Lenin's ideas were fundamentally appropriate in the early years of the Soviet Republic and are no less applicable to today's world. Lenin, Chubaryan writes, "worked out the basic strategic and tactical lines, including peaceful coexistence as a form of class struggle against the forces of imperialism and reaction." The Decree of Peace, he writes, was an early demonstration of eternal Leninism.

The decree itself called for an immediate end to hostilities in the World War I while at the same time urging the "world's toilers ... to unite their forces and drown the workers' and peasants' revolution in blood." Only in this violent way, said the decree, can the "government of bankers" be overthrown and the path laid out toward genuine peace and Socialism.

The reference to the government of bankers harkened back to Lenin's primary work on the origins of war, *Imperialism—the Highest Stage of Capitalism,* written in 1916. Current Soviet reference books, like the *Great Soviet Encyclopedia,* still describe this 60-year-old writing as a timeless "scientific analysis" that is fully applicable to the present world. The Decree of Peace, like subsequent Soviet exegeses and policies related to the war and peace question, all maintain that the foreign policy of capitalist states "assumes an aggressive and plundering character" because of the relationship that Marxism-Leninism sees between capitalism and imperialism. This simplistic formulation is bound up with the overall Manichean description in Soviet materials of two incompatible worlds—the "old world," consisting of essentially aggressive capitalist states and the "new world," to which the old is unalterably opposed, consisting of "peace-loving Socialist states."

As the peace decree and the other statements that Lenin and others indicate, the two opposing worlds are also characterized by two opposing sets of norms of international behavior—one bourgeois, the other progressively democratic and Socialist. It is said in Soviet histories and ideological tracts that the Decree of Peace was one of the first expressions of the Socialist form of international law, which is subordinate to the demands of world revolution (on the analogy of the dictatorship of the proletariat, whose revolutionary actions are "above all law"). (And in Lenin's time, as today, Soviet slogans and campaigns in the name of peace *and* Socialism have created some interesting connotations. In Russian, the word for *peace* and the word for *world* are one and the same— *mir*. Thus, when Lenin and his successors have spoken during peace campaigns of the need to extend World Socialism, they have implied that World Socialism is the same as World Peace.)

Brest-Litovsk Treaty

Before the Treaty of Brest-Litovsk was signed, Lenin had advocated peace at any price. He had calculated that this would win supporters, but, more important, he assumed that peace would bring revolution—in Russia first, then all over Europe. Of course, there was revolution in Russia and the Bolsheviks finally seized control of the country. The Germans accepted the Russians' offer to negotiate for peace because they were in a strong position against the Allies and were on their territory. Further, if they settled with the Russians, the Germans could concentrate on crushing the Western Allies. To the Allies, the offer came as a shock. They were obliged to place all their hopes in the dispatch of the American Expeditionary Force to the Continent, which occurred in the wake of the Soviet-ordered Russian withdrawal.

Negotiations with Germany opened on December 22, 1917, and lasted into March 1918. During an interruption in the talks, Lenin was outvoted by his comrades during debates at the Kremlin. Lenin stuck to his position even when the Germans began to demand that Soviet Russia give up a large slice of territory once belonging to the tsarist empire—some 150,000 square kilometers, in fact, embracing parts of Poland, Lithuania, Estonia, Latvia, the Ukraine, and Byelorussia. In his rendering of the differences among the Russian leaders over Brest-Litovsk and what Brest-Litovsk symbolizes in terms of today's Soviet foreign policy, Chubaryan describes Lenin as one of the few Soviet leaders who at that time opted for a "realistic," although compromising, peace with the Germans. He maintains that Lenin's position was well conceived, despite the unfavorable (for the Soviets) annexationist demands made by Berlin. He also says that Lenin was making a foreign-policy calculation which was based on "revolutionary" and "internationalist" factors and considerations. As the Soviet author explains, Lenin proposed his neither-war-nor-peace policy toward Germany on the basis of calculating

> ... the correlation of national and international revolutionary tasks with Soviet foreign policy; the connection between the Soviet Republic's revolutionary goals and establishment of relations with capitalist countries; the usefulness and inevitability of compromises which have to be made by a revolutionary government; and an evaluation of the tempos and perspectives of the development of the European and world-wide revolutionary process.

It was at this juncture—in early 1918—that Lenin made one of his most famous addresses on foreign policy, whose "theses," writes Chubaryan, "possess extremely great significance for the formation of Soviet foreign policy and the working out of revolutionary strategy and tactics." Lenin expressed ideas which, in nascent form, appeared in some of his prerevolutionary writings and in the Decree of Peace. The Socialist revolution at home was well underway, declared Lenin (with only partial accuracy). But then he asserted:

> The international situation in the fourth year of the war [World War I] is such that the probable outbreak of revolution and the overthrow of capitalism of some of the European imperialist governments (including the German government) cannot be counted upon.

This constituted a retreat for Lenin's position, for as recently as November 17, 1917, he had staunchly maintained, "We believe that the revolution will take place in the West." But he had also sounded a cautionary note: "We know it is inevitable, that it is impossible, of course, to create it 'on command.' ... We cannot 'issue decrees' on revolution [abroad], although we can help it along. We can help the people of the West start the victorious

Socialist revolution." At the time of the frustrating negotiations
with the Germans, Lenin was even more cautious about the
chances of revolution in the West:

> All our hopes are for the ultimate victory of Socialism, and
> they are based on both conviction as well as scientific
> prediction. Our propaganda activity as a whole and the
> fraternization drive in particular must be strengthened and
> improved. But it would be erroneous to design a tactic for the
> Socialist government of Russia which was based on the
> attempt to define whether or not the European and par-
> ticularly the German Socialist revolution would take place in
> the next six months (or in some such immediate future). It is
> impossible to make such accurate predictions, and any
> attempts to do so, objectively, only lead to dangerous gam-
> bles.

Lenin might have been subdued, but he was not abandoning
the basic premises of Soviet foreign policy, as Chubaryan shows in
quoting The Leader: Revolution was bound to come to the West;
the Soviets would continue in the future to assist in this
"inevitable" process. But in the face of the military threat then
represented by Germany, it was necessary to be flexible, and to
admit, after all, that revolutions cannot be turned on like faucets.
Moreover, without the continued existence of the "first Socialist
state," the spark which could ignite revolution would be missing.
The *first priority* consisted in protecting the Soviet Republic.
Contemporary Soviet histories of this period, like that of
Chubaryan, update the position Lenin had taken on the "correct
policy" at Brest-Litovsk by pointing out that today, too, Russia's
domestic strength and viability come first as the guarantor of
world revolution, even at the cost of making "compromises" or
temporary retreats. But compromises in terms of time and place
would by no means constitute compromising the ultimate goal of
revolution. Or as Lenin himself put it, at the time of Brest-
Litovsk:

> [We have spoken merely] of the necessity for "preparing
> and carrying out" revolutionary war. . . . We have stated this

so that we may struggle against abstract pacifism and against
the theory, in the imperialist epoch, of "defending the
[bourgeois] fatherland" ... but we have not ourselves assumed the responsibilities of beginning such revolutionary
wars without taking into account how possible it may be to
conduct them in a given place or at a given time.

Then, Lenin added the significant qualification that the revolu-
tionist must "take into account the objective *correlation of class
forces and the economic factors of the given moment for starting the
Socialist revolution.*" In the same writing, Lenin repeats the
important phrase, "correlation of class forces," which has become
so central to present-day ideological positions on world revolution
and its likelihood, based on worldwide assessments of the
contending sides, East and West. Not to take account of this
correlation, said Lenin, is to fall into "adventurism," a Marxist-
Leninist failing attributed to the Maoists, among others, by
Moscow's contemporary ideologists. The recent reiteration of this
Leninist formula quoted in Chapter One bears repeating here:

The changes in the correlation of forces in favor of
progress and Socialism and to the detriment of reaction and
imperialism are the fundamental driving force which has
created the conditions for the success of the peace initiative of
the Socialist countries, headed by the Soviet Union. They are
also the preconditions for the further struggle to get the
principles of peaceful coexistence implemented in order to
proceed successfully. The favorable development of the
balance of power on a world scale makes it possible to
combine the perspectives of the struggle for peace, democracy, and national liberation with the struggle for Socialism.

Chubaryan devotes a number of pages to recounting the
opposition which Lenin encountered when he insisted on the
policy of compromise and "tabling" revolution-by-command.
Trotsky is depicted as one of those who opposed Lenin, so also are
Bukharin, Radek, and others who were later purged under Stalin.
These "left-wing Communists," observes Churbaryan, "were
ready to accede to Soviet Russia's demise if only the European

revolution could be strengthened or unleashed." The author returns to the opposition theme when, later in his book, he discusses Lenin's policy of peaceful coexistence. He suggests here, as earlier, that perhaps today's Kremlin leadership may be divided as it was in Lenin's day on these ticklish issues.

In the final vote taken in the Central Committee on whether to sign or not the Brest-Litovsk Treaty on the harsh terms offered by the Germans, four of the "left-wing" opponents unaccountably abstained, while only two voted nay. With nine members abstaining, Lenin won by seven votes to four (among the seven was Stalin). By the terms of the treaty, signed on March 3, 1918, Russia lost most of the Ukraine, parts of the Caucasus, Poland, Finland, and the Baltic States. All of this territory had once been part of Tsarist Russia. The treaty was regarded in the West as a "Bolshevik betrayal," and it had dire repercussions for the spread of Bolshevism inside Russia, for opposition to Bolshevism was enhanced by the sell-out, the "annexationist" peace. For example, Boris Savinkov, who had been the former Provisional Government's Minister of War and who became the leader of the Socialist Revolutionaries after the Bolshevik seizure of power (the left wing of which party was just barely and only temporarily tolerated by the Bolsheviks), led an anti-Bolshevik revolt in July 1918. This revolt failed, so the Socialist Revolutionaries switched to terroristic tactics against Lenin, which resulted in Fanya (or Dora) Kaplan's unsuccessful attempt to kill the Soviet leader in 1918, and to the assassination the same day of an official of Lenin's security police, the Cheka, Moisay Uritsky. These events led immediately to the famous "Red Terror" of revenge and the seizure of hostages.

Although the Brest-Litovsk Treaty had been the evident cause of the increased spread of anti-Bolshevik feeling, both in Russia and abroad, and the immediate cause of the Red Terror, Soviet histories maintain that Lenin had made the correct decision: to save Russia for Socialism at any cost and to uphold Russian security as the first priority, not only for continuing the Socialist revolution in Russia but for assuring the future of Socialist revolution in the West, which Lenin deemed to be essential for the success of building Socialism in Russia. As to restoration of the lands taken by the Germans under the treaty, that "injustice" was to be rectified in the years to come. Some of this territory was to be reincorporated into the Soviet Union under Stalin (including parts of Poland), while post-World War II Poland was to become a Soviet satellite.

Foundation of the Third Communist International

In 1919 Lenin at last realized a lifelong dream of establishing an organization for the purpose of planning and aiding in carrying out Socialist style takeovers all over the world: the Third Communist International, or Comintern. This was established to recruit party members in other countries, consult on revolutionary and political tactics and strategy, try to suborn government or military officials in capitalist countries, and infiltrate business, labor unions, the media, universities, the League of Nations, and even religious organizations. (On commemorative dates of the seven Comintern congresses, Soviet media—especially during the Brezhnev period—traditionally hark back to the early days of the Comintern, describing Lenin's reasons for founding it as well as pointing out how Comintern goals and methods are no less applicable to today's world.)

From its very beginnings, at the first congress held from March 2 to 6, 1919, in Moscow, it was clear that Russia would dominate the Comintern's activities. This "General Staff of World Revolution," run by the Executive Committee of the Communist International (E.C.C.I.), was headed by Russians, starting with its first chief, Georgi Zinoviev. Not infrequently, Russian members of the Committee, and participants at the congresses, doubled as members of some department of the government or of the party. Such top government and/or party leaders as Lenin, Trotsky, Zinoviev, Radek, Bukharin, Tomsky, and Stalin were all, at various times, also members of the Executive Committee. This was of more than symbolic importance, for it showed that domestic political work, in the state or the party, often dovetailed with the work being performed abroad by the Comintern. (Today, certain Soviet leaders still carry on both functions, as does Party Secretary Boris N. Ponomarev. His work in the Secretariat relates to foreign Communist parties and their activities, but he also functions as a major spokesman on Soviet foreign policy, either within the Supreme Soviet or during trips abroad, as when he headed a delegation to Washington during the Brezhnev years to determine Congressional support for détente.)

Leninist Cominternism, or internationalism, was not confined in the first years to a program of making proclamations or to organizing, recognizing, or aiding and abetting Communist parties and activities abroad. At times, the Red Army was commanded by the Comintern. One such, as it turned out, ill-fated, crusade for the spread of Socialism, organized by the War Minister Trotsky, was the march on Warsaw between April and October 1920. The Soviet commander of this enterprise, Marshal Mikhail Tukhachevsky, issued an order to his troops, inspired by the Comintern, in which he proclaimed that the "destinies of world revolution will be settled ultimately in the West. Our route toward the worldwide conflagration passes over the corpse of Poland." Although on this occasion the Soviets brought along a shadow Soviet government to rule the "Soviet Poland" they expected to establish, the Polish military leader, Joseph Pilsudski, was able to halt the oncoming Red Army, just miles short of Warsaw. This rout of the Soviet army marked the end of the first attempts (other targets had included Iran) by the Soviet regime in its earlier period to use troops in order to forcibly export revolution to the West; its efforts at Sovietizing foreign lands later were confined mostly to the territories of the former tsarist empire (the "border-lands") which lay to the south and east. Some of these areas had acquired independence as the result of the March 1917 revolution in Russia which had overthrown tsarist rule and established the Provisional Government under Prince Lvov. Regardless of independence or the popular wishes of the people, Georgia, Armenia, parts of Central Asia which once formed part of the Russian empire, and far-off Outer Mongolia all in turn fell under Moscow's sway—a deliberate policy of expansion which had been initiated by Lenin, who, it is true, issued certain caveats to his more incautious commissars, and which was executed by Stalin and his henchmen at the Commissariat of Nationalities.

Despite military and other setbacks, the work of the Comintern, either in capitalist countries or in the "colonial world," by no means ceased, of course. Its activities were continued, despite a number of setbacks suffered during Lenin's life and after he died. Once the Soviet Civil War had ended, in 1921, the Russians dropped some of the international militancy in the form of direct, military intervention. By the mid-1920s, Moscow had had to watch revolutionary attempts or short-lived Soviets die in the Baltic countries, Hungary, Bulgaria, Afghanistan, Turkey, Iran, Germany, China, and elsewhere. No matter how flexible the Comintern tried to be in places such as China, where an alliance had been formed between Russian-lining Communists and the Kuomintang Nationalists, nothing seemed to work in the effort Lenin had once termed so confidently as the march to secure a "Soviet of the Whole World." As a result of frustrated attempts to export revolution, "Russia faced the indefinite prospect of remaining a lonely Communist country," as one American Soviet specialist put it. The frustrations of exporting revolution via the Red Army (as in Poland) or via the Comintern (as in Germany) influenced the Russians, under Stalin, to adopt a policy of concentrating on building Socialism "in one country" and on strengthening its military power.

During the time Stalin was in power, the Comintern was never more active. At that time, Communist parties sprang up all over the world, and Moscow's subsidies to aid in the recruitment of members, opening of newspapers, paying of bail to release imprisoned comrades, and so on were by no means niggardly. By the early 1930s in the United States, for example, there were well-known intellectuals who were influenced into thinking that Communist Russia was the wave of the future, a truly progressive country. Communist youth organizations functioned, sometimes effectively, in the larger European and American cities, and even in smaller towns. Pamphlets, newspapers, demonstrations, strikes, and "popular-front" activities running the gamut from penetration of political parties to school clubs, the latter seemingly lacking an overt political function, all were part of the "legal" activity the Comintern sponsored that was visible in any capitalist country in the 1920s and 1930s. Not so visible were illegal activities, whether planned or actually executed, nor was the system for communicating the orders from Moscow to these fifth columns. Two notorious events on the level of Soviet domestic and foreign policy interfered with the effectiveness of the Comintern in the West under Stalin, which was expected to work in tandem with Soviet foreign policy. One was the purge trials of the late 1930s, news of which leaked out slowly, but when it was finally believed and assimilated by the intelligentsia of the West, its effect was devastating. The second, more potent blow to the Comintern and to fellow-traveling leftists was Stalin's decision to conclude a nonaggression pact with Hitler, which included trade and political ties and whose ramifications were most damaging to the anti-Fascist cause in the West (the new friendliness with Germany was symbolized by Molotov's congratulatory message to Hitler upon the *Wehrmacht's* capture of Paris in June 1940). The decision also was counterproductive for the popular-front movement. With the German attack on the Soviet Union of June 1941 and the hasty formation of an anti-Axis alliance between East and West, the Comintern became an embarrassment.

A curious misconception about the Comintern has existed in the West since World War II. Some people consider that because Stalin dissolved the Leninist Comintern in 1943 that a Communist "International" no longer exists. True, the Comintern, the Profintern (trade-union Comintern), the Executive Committee of the Communist International, the Sovintern (Soviet branch of the Comintern), even the Cominform (the Communist Information Bureau which was the official successor to the Comintern from 1950 to 1956) and the Sovinformburo (Soviet branch of the Cominform) no longer exist. Despite this, Cominternism still exists, and along with it, a cryptic International. Moreover, the corresponding structures, organs, and officials of the Central Committee of the Soviet Communist party remain to carry out the tasks that once belonged to the actual Comintern of Lenin's or Stalin's day. For example, Secretary Boris Ponomarev, promoted in 1976 to alternate member of the Politburo, once worked in the Executive Committee between 1937 and 1943 and from 1946 to 1949 headed the Sovinformburo, or the Soviet branch of the Cominform. Since 1953, Ponomarev has been in charge of relations of the Russian Communist party with foreign Communist parties through the corresponding department of the Central Committee. This office and its functions double with those of the foreign departments of the K.G.B.'s "First Chief Directorate," which is responsible for all Soviet clandestine activities in foreign countries. Like the Comintern, but in far more elaborate and clandestine fashion than in the days of the Comintern,

Ponomarev's Central Committee office, the K. G. B., and to a lesser extent the G. R. U. (military intelligence) carry out functions which are identical to the Third International: recruitment of Communist party members in other countries; consultation on revolutionary and political tactics and strategy; efforts to suborn government or military personnel of capitalist countries; penetration of offices in capitalist business, labor unions, the media, universities, the UN Secretariat, and even religious organizations. One of the principal tasks of the First Chief Directorate is to issue clandestinely erroneous information about alleged "trends" inside the Kremlin or the "true meaning" of an official policy. This work is carried out by the K. G. B.'s Disinformation Department, one of the most important, if oddly named, affiliates of the First Chief Directorate. Another important function of Ponomarev's section, but less so of the K. G. B., is standardizing Communist tactics and strategy, the party line and the public message of the Russian Communist party with those of the foreign Communist parties, whether ruling or not. Since the death of Stalin, this activity, initiated and guided by Moscow, has been complicated by the phenomenon of "polycentrism," "Eurocentrism," and other signs of centrifugality, or the drawing of parties away from Moscow. Communist countries, too, are involved in propagating centrifugality: Tito's Yugoslavia, Communist China, and Albania are such examples. The Communist parties of France, Spain, Italy, and of other Western countries (excluding that of the United States, however) have displayed a strong urge for increasing autonomy, less Muscovite autocracy of the type enforced through Ponomarev, the Central Committee, and the K. G. B. and which was recently reasserted at the 25th Party Congress in 1976.*

After the Comintern

The dissolution of the Comintern in 1943 is described in the Moscow Higher Party School textbook as follows:

* See discussion of the June 1976 conference of the 29 European Communist parties below, pp. 170-171.

Wartime conditions demanded of the Communist parties, the majority of whom had been converted into experienced, militant, and influential parties able independently to adopt Marxist-Leninist strategy and tactics, that the forms of struggle be changed, that the parties learn how to maneuver, retreat, and wage offensives. The Comintern, therefore, had fulfilled its historical function of lending ideological and tactical strength to the world Communist movement and in working out its ideological and tactical principles. Under such conditions, the leadership of the Communist movement from a single center less and less corresponded to the real situation. As a result, the Presidium of the E. C. C. I. issued the decree of May 15, 1943, to dissolve the Communist International ... The Comintern's dissolution thereupon created the best possible conditions for uniting all the progressive forces in each country into a single national-liberation, anti-Fascist front and helped, too, to unite all freedom-loving peoples into a single anti-Fascist coalition. Also, the Comintern's dissolution exposed the Fascist lie alleging that "Moscow" intended to interfere in the internal affairs of other countries for the purpose of "Bolshevizing" them. Dissolving of the Comintern not only did not weaken but, on the contrary, facilitated the organizing of a mighty anti-Fascist people's struggle.

The book continues in the next paragraph to evaluate—with unqualified affirmation—the whole activity of the Comintern between 1919 and 1943 as a "world-historical" heritage from which *much can be learned today and whose world-historical strategic and tactical schemes are still valid.*

In the book's next section, discussing the work of the united anti-Fascist organizations and parties, the various underground activities that were carried out both during World War II and in the immediate postwar period by anti-Nazi movements and other organizations that were similar to the Comintern in the European countries are recounted. This movement, says the textbook, would have resulted in the establishment of Soviet Socialist regimes in the West European countries under German occupation had it not been for the "Anglo-American armed forces."

This struggle would have developed into Socialist revolution had it not been for the Normandy landings of the Anglo-American armed forces, who thereupon helped to install into power a bourgeois government, while the working class considered, as its most important goal, the ending of the anti-Fascist war.

The textbook then contrasts this frustration of Socialist revolution in the West with the successful attainment of Socialism in the East (in Central and Southeastern Europe) with the help of the Soviet Army, where the "anti-Fascist struggle became a popular front headed by the working class which was in turn led by the Communists in the form of a struggle by partisans." The Sovietization of the various countries of this area is discussed, and then the problem of Italy is compared to that of France:

In Italy conditions were such that a people's revolution could have been made. But here, as in France, the Anglo-American armed forces helped to install a bourgeois order, preventing the conversion of a liberation struggle into a Socialist revolution in Italy.

The lesson learned from the Communist failure in Western countries to unleash the Socialist revolution, according to the textbook, consists of realizing the presence of "schism in the ranks of the international working class." The Social Democrats, it says, pursued a policy of anti-Sovietism and anti-Communism, both before as well as after the war. Western trade unions, too, were guilty of dividing the working class. These phenomena weakened Communist activism just as the "second phase" in the "crisis of capitalism" began (see chart, p. 65). After the war, says the book, a new revolutionary situation arose in a "number of the European [obviously, West European] countries." Just at this time, in the early postwar period, it became necessary for European Communists to recall Lenin's advice as to the difference between the tactics to be employed by Communists in this or another country in a revolutionary situation, but, more importantly, to the *similarities in those tactics:*

At the same time, the experience of all countries entering upon the road to Socialism showed that general laws for making the Socialist revolution and for building Socialism applied equally and were equally obligatory for each and every country, laws which also formed the objective basis for strengthening the Socialist Commonwealth.

Later on, Brezhnev is quoted in the same vein. The present Soviet leader advocates "universal" revolutionary tactics and strategy which are applicable to all countries, regardless of differing local conditions, which, however, must be taken into account for fine-tuning of tactics.

Foundation of the Cominform

The need for the creation of the Communist Information Bureau (Cominform) in 1947 is described as follows, in the Higher Party School textbook:

Immediately after the end of World War II, monopolistic capital took the offensive against the vital interests of the toilers. The imperialist ruling circles began preparations for a new world war. Under these conditions, the need became entirely obvious to renew and to strengthen contacts between the Marxist-Leninist parties and to set up a means for exchanging their experience. After the dissolution of the Comintern, no such international Communist organ existed. Thus, it became necessary for Communists to *find some new forms of multifaceted ties.* The first attempt at establishing these links was the Communist Information Bureau, whose first session held in Warsaw in September 1947 included representatives from the CPs of the USSR, Poland, Czecho-slovakia, Bulgaria, Hungary, Rumania, Yugoslavia, France and Italy. . . . It was unanimously agreed that *two camps had come into existence—the imperialist, anti-democratic camp . . . and the anti-imperialist, democratic camp. . . . Between the two camps a fierce struggle was taking place whose intensity grew along with the deepening of the general crisis of capitalism* [as capitalism began to enter its third and last phase of crisis in the mid-1950s] and the *weakening of the forces of capitalism and the strengthening of the forces of Socialism and democracy.* . . . The U.S.A. and the other imperialist nations entered on the path of forming aggressive military blocs, of economic expansion, and of strengthening the ideological struggle. The U.S. began to carry out its plan to convert West Germany and Japan into weapons of imperialists counted upon divisions in the ranks of the working class. . . . [The Cominform dedicated itself to] cutting off the plans of the American aggressors. . . . The task of the Communist parties consisted in taking the lead in opposing monopoly-capitalism and forging around this opposition all democratic and patriotic forces on the basis of a common anti-imperialist and democratic platform.

The text describes the various political and editorial activities of the Cominform, or the "collective forms of cooperation" achieved during the nine years of organization until its disbanding in April 1956. This dissolution of the "second Comintern" is explained on the basis of the following rationale:

The development of the revolutionary process throughout the world confronted Communists with the task of broadening their collective forms of cooperation. It also became necessary to reconstruct mutual Communist party relations by taking into account the new stage in their development and maturity. The necessity thus arose for new forms of ties between the Communist parties. In April 1956 Cominform participants [nine parties] recognized that the Cominform had fulfilled its functions and decided by mutual agreement to stop its activities and the publication of the newspaper, *For a Lasting Peace, for a People's Democracy.*

The World Conference Route

The new stage in the world revolutionary movement which opened in the second half of the 1950s demanded of the Communist parties that they study the new conditions obtaining throughout the world and solve the newly-ripened problems in the struggle for peace, democracy, national freedom, and Socialism, an important contribution to which was made by the CPSU 20th Party Congress (1956).

The book then turns to the new organizational forms of Cominternism and Cominformism. It describes this stage as taking form of the three conferences of the world's Communist and Workers' parties held in Moscow in 1957, 1960, and 1969 (and the "fourth conference" of which is long overdue, quite possibly because the Russian Communist party has now decided that a new Comintern-Cominform should be formed, but its little-sister parties worldwide have by no means agreed on just what organizational form this new structure should assume). Toward the end of the textbook, the implication is made that such an organization, that is, the successor to the Comintern and Cominform, is long overdue, since the "generality of the aims and tasks" of the world's Communists has never been more evident than in the present, last stage of the crisis of capitalism. "At present," the book asserts, "the international movement of the adherents to Communism is *not facilitated by any form of chartered organization, nor does there exist a single organizational center* [*in the geographic sense*] *as existed at the time of the Comintern. Nevertheless, the Communist movement is not the mere sum of separate parties isolated from each other;* it is a voluntary union of equal, independent Communist parties which *are bound together by the ties of proletarian, Socialist internationalism; a single ideology; by the common struggle against a common enemy, imperialism, and toward the single goal of communism.*" One is reminded here of the rationale for a single organizational center found in the theses of the Second Congress of the Comintern in 1920:

The world political situation has now placed the proletarian dictatorship on the order of the day, and all events in world politics are necessarily concentrated at one central point [the Russian Soviet Republic] which is rallying round itself both the Soviet movements among advanced workers in all countries, and all national-liberation movements in the colonies and among oppressed peoples.

And, from the same congress:

> The Communist International recognizes that in order to hasten victory, the Workingmen's Association, which is fighting to annihilate capitalism and create communism, must have a strongly centralized organization. The Communist International must, in fact and in deed, be a single Communist party of the entire world. The parties working in the various countries are but its separate detachments. The organizational machinery of the Communist International must guarantee the workers of each country the opportunity of getting the utmost help from the organized proletariat of other countries at any given moment.

From the Fourth Congress of the Comintern, December 1922:

> This procedure gives the Communist International, as a centralized world party, the opportunity of transmitting to individual parties from "above to below," by means of democratic centralism, directives based on international experience as a whole.

It is noteworthy that while the Cominform functioned mainly as a *European* Communist organization, the world-conference procedures followed by Communist parties between 1957 and 1969 have embraced Communist or pro-Communist parties all over the globe. These conferences and their resultant declarations and "theses" more nearly resemble the Comintern than the transitional Cominform. Putting it another way, it is apparent that a major reason why the Cominform was disbanded in 1956 was that its activities were too limited. Moreover, it is significant that the birth of the world conferences in 1957 paralleled the renascence of Cominternist ideology at the 20th Congress and in the new Program of the Soviet Communist party, which was being drafted in those years and which was finally approved by the upper councils of the party in 1961.

These years also paralleled the opening of what Soviet ideologists call the "third stage" in the "general crisis of capitalism," a stage marked by intensification of the worldwide class struggle; by the development of an allegedly favorable correlation of forces for the Communists; by the central importance of the peace plank (peaceful coexistence, relaxation of tension, and prevention of a new world war); and by national-liberation struggles in the colonial or newly independent countries located in areas sensitive to Western economic and/or military interests. It is frequently maintained today by Soviet spokesmen and their allies in the Soviet Bloc that this "last" stage in the decline and fall of capitalism is so crucial that something more than world conferences is needed to meet the demands of the times. They often complain that factionalism (of "left" and "right") prevents unification of the world proletarian movement. Were this disunity overcome and true "internationalism" under Moscow's hegemony restored, they maintain, a new world organization, resembling the old Comintern, could be established. Meanwhile, the worldwide "Communist mission" will have to be effected through these world conferences, by means of links between the Central Committee of the Soviet Communist party and foreign "detachments" and, above all, by means of a dynamic foreign policy which not only does not ignore but is greatly motivated by basic ideological demands.

Khrushchev speaks in his memoirs of the double purpose of the Soviet policy (the "double-track" characteristic of Soviet foreign policy) with respect to Egypt in 1956. He writes that under Stalin, the possibilities for Soviet penetration in the Near East, and Egypt in particular, had been missed in the past because Stalin had insisted that the "Near East was part of Britain's sphere of influence and that therefore we couldn't go sticking our nose in Egypt's affairs." He continues:

Not that Stalin wouldn't have liked to move into the Near East—he would have liked to very much—but he realistically recognized that the balance of power wasn't in our favor and that Britain wouldn't have stood for our interference.

Things changed during the intervening years. Our economy, our armed forces, and the weight of our influence in international affairs all increased mightily, and by 1956 we were able to step in and assist President Nasser and the Arab peoples.

Then, Khrushchev frames this "stepping in" within the context of Soviet Cominternism, or what is called today, the mission of "internationalism":

We weren't motivated by self-centered, mercantile interests. Quite the contrary, we wanted only to help these peoples to cast off the yoke of their servile dependence on their colonialist masters. Ours has been a noble mission in the Near East. We have incorporated into our diplomacy the tenets of Lenin's own foreign policy, and we have already begun to reap the fruits of our investment in the future of the Arab nations.

One of the most recent reiterations of Cominternism, of merging ideological/revolutionary goals with foreign policy, assumed the innocuous form of two book reviews in *Pravda* and *Izvestia.* The book was *History of the Foreign Policy of the USSR* (1976), a highly authoritative work under the joint editorship of Foreign Minister Andrei Gromyko and the Soviet Communist Party Secretary Boris Ponomarev. The two reviews differed somewhat, but in the key "internationalist" section of each of them, the "message" had been carefully written and edited. In *Pravda*'s review, the writer, V. N. Nekrasov, chief of the European desk of the newspaper, asserted that

Respect for the right of each people to select its own path of development is the unshakable principle of Soviet foreign policy. But here, as everywhere else, the Soviet Union comes forward on the side of the forces of progress, democracy, and national independence.

The key word "but" is significantly retained in the second review as well, which appeared ten days later in *Izvestia* under the byline of the authoritative columnist, Nikolai Polyanov. *Izvestia*'s version of the section went as follows:

Our country does not interfere in the internal affairs of other countries and peoples. *But* we do not conceal our views. In the developing countries, as everywhere else, we stand by the side of the forces of progress, democracy and national independence.*

The Genoa Conference

This was Soviet Russia's first meeting with the West, in 1922. Lenin himself had been invited by Western officials, in the hopes that he would head the Russian delegation. For a time, it did look as if he would avail himself of this opportunity to make a personal charismatic "invasion" of the West. But for some reason— probably having to do with both health and the press of domestic politics—Lenin decided not to go to Italy.

The intent of the conference was ostensibly to discuss post-World War I economic reconstruction. The Soviets had been invited because even West European conservatives, of the type of the British Prime Minister, Lloyd George, had become aware of the fact that the Soviet government was apparently here to stay. The Bolsheviks had won their civil war, and moreover now seemed embarked on an internal policy of making concessions to private enterprise (the New Economic Policy) coupled to looking to the West for trade and diplomatic relations. A phase in "normalizing" relations with the West was obviously beginning, the first of a series of normalizations that have taken place in these relations. True, a good deal of this "retreat" had been forced upon Moscow. For one thing, militant Cominternism and the use of the Red Army to export Communism abroad had largely failed. Marshal Pilsudski had repelled the invading Soviet forces in 1920. Soviet thrusts in the direction of the Baltic countries and westward along the southern extension of its western border, either in the form of overt troop movements or by means of exported subversion, had also failed. Gripped with famine, disease, and ruin and disruption following the Civil War, Soviet Russia under Lenin began to turn its attention away from "world revolution" (that is, in terms of *priorities)* and to domestic rehabilitation. Although the Soviet leader by no means lost hope for an eventual

* It may be significant, in documenting the moderate trend in Soviet policy setting in after spring 1976 (see below, pp. 169-171), that the No. 8 May issue of *Kommunist* contained a review of the book which omitted the "but" phrase.

revolutionary overturn of the Western "bourgeois order," he began in 1921 to speak of the remoteness of this event. Moreover, Lenin and his colleagues reasoned that they could best deflect the Western urge either to undo Bolshevism or to encircle it by doing business with the West, and creating an image of respectability. "The bourgeois countries must trade with Russia," said Lenin. "We must trade with the capitalist nations, as long as they exist as such."

Contemporary Soviet descriptions of Lenin's readjustment of Soviet priorities in the early 1920s quote the founder of the Soviet state to the effect that Russia needed a "breathing spell" at the time of the Genoa Conference in order to reconstruct itself. Lenin is also said to have regarded Russian participation in the conference as an opportunity to make propaganda for the new regime and lend support to the foreign workers' movement. This would take the form of a bold, if hypocritical, stand on universal disarmament and the "bourgeois-pacifist" program. Also, statements would be issued (during the Conference) calculated to win influence among the French and British working classes and to exert indirect pressure in this way on the "bourgeois" governments of those countries. Moreover, Lenin hoped to acquire a sizeable loan from the West "which was of extreme necessity for Soviet Russia."

As it turned out, the main business of the Genoa Conference brought few tangible results, and no major loan for Soviet Russia. But another development did take place which had enormous importance: the Rapallo Treaty with Germany. Lenin had instructed the People's Commissariat of Foreign Affairs to open secret talks with the Germans months before Genoa. The main purpose of this was the traditional Leninist goal of dividing the West, of somehow detaching Germany from the rest of Europe and thereby weakening the West. Behind this stood another purpose: to bring revolution to Germany, a country which had always enjoyed a high priority in Moscow's internationalist, Cominternist strategy. To win Germany's affections, Moscow was prepared to support revisions of the Treaty of Versailles in Germany's favor; the Soviets began to refer to the treaty as the "annexationist" Versailles treaty. So, during the multilateral discussions at Genoa, the Soviet delegation, headed by the able and experienced Soviet diplomat and Commissar of Foreign Affairs, George Chicherin, won a secret audience with the German delegation. The two sides sat down at the conference table in the neighboring village of Rapallo and quietly went over the draft of a treaty worked out months before in Berlin. On April 16, 1922, the historic treaty was signed, thus opening a long period of collaboration that lasted from 1922 to 1941. During this time, the two countries cooperated economically and militarily, despite the tension that arose between Soviet *Realpolitik* (promoting national interests) and Comintern support for the German Communists; despite the analogous tension created between Soviet *government* aid to the right-wing German militarists and *Comintern* encouragement of the left-wing German Communist and the pro-Communist left within the ranks of the Social Democrats.

That "other topic" at Genoa was to be disarmament, but the Western Allies had decided that this would not be a fruitful agenda item and that the conference should concentrate on economics. However, the Russians became aware of this, and Lenin and his colleagues discussed, in Politburo meetings before the conference, how they would go to the Western conference to try to normalize relations, get a loan for Russia, *but* also make propaganda about disarmament, prodding and embarrassing the Western powers in the process. Pacifist slogans, said Lenin, would attract the world's attention to the Soviet republic and embarrass the capitalist powers represented at the conference. "We, as Communists, have *our* Communist program (the Third International), *but* we regard it as our duty as merchants [at the conference] to *support* (even on a one in ten thousand chance) the *pacifists* in the OTHER, that is, the bourgeois camp. . . . This will be venomous as well as 'friendly' and will contribute to the demoralization of the enemy. With such tactics we shall gain *even* if Genoa fails." Lenin went on to describe the political exploitation of "bourgeois pacifism" (in his instructions to the Soviet Genoa delegation):

The pacifist wing [of the English bourgeoisie] we must consider as petty-bourgeois, pacifist, or semi-pacifist democracy of the type of Keynes, etc. . . . One of the principal if not the main political aims at Genoa should be to divide this [pacifist] wing from the rest of the bourgeois camp; to try to flatter this wing; to assert that it is quite acceptable from our point of view to reach not only trade but also political agreement with it.

Do everything possible, even what may be impossible, in order to strengthen the pacifist wing of the bourgeoisie so as to increase even slightly its chances of victory in the elections. This is primary, but secondly, to divide among themselves the bourgeois countries ranged against us at Genoa—this is our two-pronged political aim at Genoa. In no way frame all this within a Communist point of view.

... By all means, deeply split the pacifist camp of the petty-bourgeoisie away from the crude-bourgeoisie, from the aggressive-bourgeoisie, and the reactionary-bourgeoisie.

The author, Chubaryan, comments candidly at the end of these quotations from Lenin's instructions: *"The pacifist program, therefore, was a form of class struggle, a tactic used by the Socialist country in the struggle against the reactionary bourgeoisie."*

A private letter addressed by Lenin to Chicherin, and only recently released by the Marx-Engels-Lenin Institute in Moscow, contains Lenin's "corrections and remarks" on a speech that the Soviet Foreign Affairs Commissar was to deliver in Genoa. The Soviet leader reveals the *"diopezza,"* double-tiered, sense in which he viewed the "peace slogan." Lenin told Chicherin to use no "frightening words" in his address, above all, to strike out any reference to revolutionary "use of violent means." Furthermore, Lenin said, do not refer to the "unavoidability of new wars"; this phrase must be "unconditionally thrown out." Instead of referring to the "bloody struggle" to attain Socialism, Lenin wrote, "remember that we are coming here as 'merchants.'" Lenin's remarks set a precedent for his successors to follow, particularly after the death of Stalin. For he was devising statements for Western consumption designed to enhance Soviet respectability, to win financial credits, trade, and so on, but which were deliberately worded to conceal basic Communist or Cominternist tactics and strategy.

In *V.I. Lenin and the Formation of Soviet Foreign Policy,* the author, Chubaryan speaks of the consistency of Lenin's foreign policy at this time with Communist internationalism, even while Lenin sought to open a trade window to the West and to normalize relations with the West in a time of "ebb" in the world-revolutionary process. "In terms of the world-revolutionary process," Chubaryan asserts, "the program advanced by the Soviet government at Genoa [reduction of armaments and outlawing war as a means of settling disputes] had invaluable importance." It was designed to strengthen the world's first Socialist state, "whose existence was the indispensable premise for the successful development of the world-revolutionary movement." By putting forward his program for peaceful relations with capitalism, the book states, "Lenin did not desist in defending and propagandizing Communist principles. ... He put forward the idea of convening all-world congresses, participated in by workers' organizations, which would call for revision of the League of Nations charter and other proposals aimed at increasing the representation of the toiling masses in world organizations. The policy of peaceful coexistence was an important means whereby the positions of the revolutionary forces could be strengthened while the positions of imperialism could be weakened. The peaceful coexistence policy was thus a form of class struggle against the forces of imperialism and reaction." Although Chubaryan's book is an obvious instance of what historians call present-interest history, or viewing the past against the demands and biases of the present, there is little doubt that Lenin *did* view the usefulness of the Genoa Conference mainly from the standpoint of national interest (giving the Soviet republic a breathing spell), while also making a first trial of the principle of peaceful coexistence as a "form of class struggle."

In discussing the "Leninist origins" of the policy of peaceful coexistence, present-day Soviet materials not only hark back to the 1922 Genoa Conference but to still earlier, somewhat vague references by Lenin to coexistence. However, coexistence had been largely a compromise forced upon Soviet Russia by several circumstances after 1920. First, world, or even European, revolution did not break out and spread as Lenin and his colleagues expected it would, or at least said it would, between 1917 and 1920. The Bolsheviks surely did all they could, even under conditions of civil war at home, to promote world revolution. In the case, for example, of the Baltic States of Estonia, Latvia, Lithuania, and Finland, they were prepared to tear up the self-determination promises of the Provisional Government issued after the overthrow of the tsar in March 1917. Subversion and attempts at Sovietization were not only made against these states but against the independent nations of the Ukraine, Georgia, Armenia, and Azerbaidjan. In some places, like the Baltic States, Soviet republics were established for a time, until the local populations and the legal governments were able to disband them; in other places, like the Ukraine, the Caucasus, and Central Asia, the Soviet republics became permanent. Second, there seemed to be no prospects, in the immediate future at least, for the further military export of Soviet Communism, either in the areas where it had been attempted and failed, or in areas farther west in Europe. Moreover, the Soviet Civil War had brought chaos to the country, necessitating a concentration on rebuilding the country above all else. For this purpose, Western help would be needed, as in the case of the American Relief Administration, under the chairmanship of Herbert Hoover, which had been permitted to come into Soviet Russia to dole out $20 million in food and medicine to the masses (as a result, about 10,000,000 people were saved by this American enterprise according to George Kennan's estimate).

Peaceful coexistence, under Lenin as well as his successor, Stalin, began to be interpreted as a way of attaining a breathing spell for Russian rehabilitation, and later, for industrialization and collectivization as well as military buildup. Through the normalization policies of peaceful coexistence, Russia might remain free of "bourgeois imperialist meddling" (by means of what Stalin called the "capitalist encirclement" of Russia) while at the same time opening useful business contacts with the West and establishing a respectable Soviet presence in capitalist countries.

Finally, the Comintern would continue to serve as a source of fifth-column subversion in capitalist countries, a means of accomplishing what the Red Army obviously could not. Viewed from a geopolitical point of view, the Comintern, with its affiliates worldwide, provided land-locked Russia with a form of egress out into the rest of the world. It was not until the 1960s that Soviet rockets could achieve "astronautical" egress, and not until the 1970s when the Soviet navy was beginning to be designed for naval egress. In short, Cominternism became Stalin's and his successors' means by which Russia could puncture and penetrate the alleged capitalist encirclement, providing remote Russia with the accessibility to Western industrial nations and Western colonies which geography alone could not provide her.

Puncturing and penetrating the capitalist world and overthrowing the capitalist order by means of subversion, rather than outright force of arms, have special meaning in the present age of thermonuclear weapons. In Chapter One, we saw that certain Soviet spokesmen, including military men who evidently followed instructions from civilian ideologists, could describe a future world conflict as a "continuation of politics by other means." In *Marxism-Leninism on War and Army,* pacifists were rebuked for regarding nuclear war as "unthinkable"; other writers from the Soviet bloc have complained about the pacifists' "fetishism" over thermonuclear weapons, their ruling out of nuclear war as an "unjust" and "unacceptable" conflict. We also saw how this Soviet view has been contended in the Yugoslav Communist press (see above, p. 25 and below, pp. 158-161). The export of revolution by rocket also has its critics, apparently, inside the ruling structures of Soviet bloc countries. For example, K.G.B. Chief Yuri Andropov, a leading representative of the use of subversives inside Russia as well as abroad, strongly attacked militarism and the continuing "waste of material resources" on arms. Andropov also described the "catastrophic consequences" of tilting on the edge of thermonuclear war or of engaging in such a conflict. Ruling out the unlikely possibility that Mr. Andropov, heir to the tradition of the Cheka, Yagoda, and Beria, had suddenly become a pacifist, we are left with another, more convincing inference. The implications of Andropov's antimilitarist diatribe are that the export of revolution by means of nuclear arms is too dangerous in the present age. As intelligence chief and administrator of a vast global army of subversives, Andropov was obliquely commending the use of the Comintern to spread Socialism as the method less fraught with catastrophic consequences. Besides urging this means of attaining world revolution, Andropov may also have been attacking the "Tukhachevskyists," that is, those militaristically-inclined Communists (some of whom wear military uniforms) who do not demur in the face of the ultimate weapons, and who would risk world war with local wars in the interests of Socialism. This also was suggested by the East German Minister of Defense and Politburo member, General Heinz Hoffmann. There is even some evidence for the appearance of an antimilitarist trend in the Soviet Union following the twin deaths of Marshal A. A. Grechko and General S. M. Shtemenko in April 1976. In the spring of 1976, a welter of references to "catastrophic consequences" (in the context of a third world war) and the hazards of a policy of "confrontation" between the superpowers were made in Soviet media. This in turn suggested that war as a means of disseminating Socialism, or even the ongoing arms buildup in the Soviet Union, was meeting opposition within the Russian Communist party. It was too early to tell whether the opposition was directed ultimately against General Secretary and Marshal Brezhnev or whether it was not related to the "civilianization" of the Soviet Ministry of Defense.

Early East-West Peaceful Coexistence

The 1920s saw Lenin's Russia opening a variety of windows to the West. Peace and friendship treaties, diplomatic recognition, trade deals, but notably *not* Soviet membership in the League of Nations (until 1934 when the Russians decided to join), all accompanied the first Soviet expression of peaceful coexistence. Not infrequently, Western countries that had decided to normalize their relations with Soviet Russia found themselves threatened by the Comintern's fifth columns, for whom normal diplomatic relations proved helpful in gaining entry into and stepping up their activities in the bourgeois countries. For example, in 1923 the German government obtained proof that the Soviet embassy in Berlin was exploiting its diplomatic status there to purchase arms for a Bolshevik-style revolution plotted by the Executive Committee back in Moscow. In Britain, too, there were difficulties. British recognition of the Bolshevik regime was called an

"historic step" by the Second Congress of Soviets in 1924, and
Chicherin praised the sagacity of the "best section of the English
ruling circles" for their decision. But relations with Britain would
vary, depending upon the extent to which it was evident that the
Soviets were plotting revolution in that country. In October 1924,
the revolutionary "Zinoviev letter," possibly apocryphal, actually
led to the downfall of the Labour Government headed by Ramsay
MacDonald. Documents of the Fifth and Sixth Congresses of the
Communist International (1924 and 1928) make it unmistakably
clear that Cominternism would not be in the least affected by
peaceful coexistence between the East and West, trade, normalization, or treaties of friendship.

During the Fifth Congress, for example, a special Comintern
Executive Committee resolution was issued that referred to the
newly elected Labour Government in Britain as an "event of the
greatest significance." Class consciousness had been awakened in
that country, the resolution continued, and the time had arrived
for starting a "revolutionary struggle ... since the Labour
Government is not a government of proletarian class struggle
[and] aspires to strengthen the bourgeois state system by reforms
and by class peace." The means used by the British Communist
party to realize the proletarian revolution included slogans
"designed to mobilize the class-conscious section of the working
masses for joint action ... to plant its organization deep among
the revolutionary working masses, above all, at their place of
work." The thrust of the resolution was largely along lines of
"popular-front" building "from below," to publicize Communist
demands while placing Communists in key positions, so that when
the "revolutionary situation" developed (as instructed by Lenin in
The Infantile Disease of Leftwing Communism), Communists
would be in a position to carry out a revolutionary takeover. In
the manifesto of the Fifth Congress, written by Trotsky and issued
in July 1924, came this characterization of the normalization of
relations between East and West: "The growth of the Communist
parties consolidates the international position of the Soviet Union
while it troubles and angers the imperialists. When the direct
danger of revolution rises again, the imperialists may once more
turn to large-scale military intervention. . . . Between the capitalist
world and Soviet Republic agreements are possible, but not

reconciliation . . . [since] different interests may and will cut across the agreements of capitalist countries with the Soviet Union. That is why the Red Army and the Red Navy are necessary." Meanwhile, "We have to seize power and guide it along Socialist channels. If Soviet Russia was able over a number of years to stand out against capitalist Europe and America together, the victory of the European proletariat will be the more certain when, after capturing power, the states of Europe come together in a Soviet Federation, the United Workers' and Peasants' States of Europe."

The Sixth Congress of the Comintern in 1928, also in the era of Soviet Russia's "coming into the world," was attended by 575 delegates representing 4 million Communists, or a half million more than were represented at the Fifth Congress. Sixty-six parties and organizations were invited to the proceedings in Moscow which lasted from July 17 to September 1. Like the Fifth, the Sixth Congress constituted a reaffirmation of Cominternism, but was also the occasion for the adoption of the most comprehensive set of rules and basic principles in Comintern history, in the form of the Constitution and Rules of the Communist International and the Program of the Third International. Examination of these documents shows that in the various tactics (the "United Front," for example), and in terms of strategy, nothing had changed since the first Leninist congress of 1919, despite the era of normalization of relations between East and West, peaceful coexistence, and bilateral treaties between the Soviet Union and numerous Western countries. Lest these references to "remote" Comintern congresses seem anachronistic to the general reader, let him ponder this very recent *Pravda* interpretation (of April 8, 1976) of what the policy of peaceful coexistence means for latterday Cominternism:

It is time to understand that peaceful coexistence extends to inter-state relations. It does not replace, nor could it replace, the laws of class struggle, of the liberation movement, and of social progress.

Between the Sixth and Seventh Congresses of the Comintern (1928 and 1935) were seven years of "frustration" for the world-revolutionary process and movement. These were the years of distractive internecine struggle within the Kremlin, when Stalin finally won his fight against the "rightist" deviation of Bukharin, Rykov, and Tomsky; of the industrial dislocations and struggle under the First Five-year Plan (1928 to 1932); the widespread liquidations and privations suffered under the policy of forcible collectivization of agriculture (between 1927 and 1933); and the famines of 1931 and 1933. These events explain why Soviet diplomacy was mostly used for defensive purposes between the years of recognition, between 1922 and 1924 and the advent of Hitler in 1933. The Soviets well understood, and understand today, that the politics of revolution is the art of the possible.

STAGES OF THE "GENERAL CRISIS OF CAPITALISM" *

First Stage

1917 - 1939

October Revolution:
—beginning of era of first anti-imperialist revolutions and of irreversible processes leading to fall of capitalism
—establishment of the Comintern

Second Stage

1939 - 1956

World War II starts transition to Second Stage:
—overthrow of capitalism in E. Europe with formation of first World Socialist System

---

* Source: *Mezhdunarodnoye Kommunisticheskoye, Rabocheye i Natsional'no-Osvoboditel'noye Dvizheniye* (International Communist Workers' and National Liberation Movement), Moscow, 1974.

—further weakening of positions held by imperialism
—sharpening of inner capitalist contradictions, abetted by international Socialist-vs-capitalist struggle
—rise of national-liberation movement as collapse of imperialism's colonial system begins
—hostile capitalist encirclement

Third Stage

1956-1970s

"Last, decisive battle for overthrow of capitalism and for Socialism draws near" (Brezhnev):
—more countries attain Socialism without world war
—hope for revolution spreads to middle classes
—"étatization" of monopolies and militarization of capitalist societies
—stepped-up class struggle, polarization of capital and labor, militarist *vs.* peace forces
—new correlation of forces alters and disarms capitalist encirclement

3

The Stalinist Prelude to Détente

The death of Josef Stalin is customarily, and by and large, accurately, regarded as the major turning point in recent Soviet history. Foreign policy, of course, was bound to be affected by the abrupt end of the 25-year reign of the powerful dictator, the "continuer of the work of Lenin." And a number of changes in foreign policy were made. But it can also be argued quite convincingly that a number of policies that were begun within weeks after his death in March 1953 had been contemplated, and explicitly so, by Stalin. It is worthwhile exploring this point, not only to set the record straight, but to gain an appreciation of the continuity of Soviet policy and grand strategy.

Near the end, Stalin appears to have been in another of his moods to make major changes in domestic and foreign policy and in ideology. In the past, when "objective conditions" called for policy overhauls, agonizing reappraisals and resultant new policies emerged from the Kremlin. Thus, new policies were announced at the time of the death of Lenin and the interregnum jockeying for power during the next four years; worldwide depression beginning in the late 1920s; erupting tensions in the Far East between China and Japan, and between Russia and

Japan, and Russia and China; the spread of fascism in central Europe, culminating in the accession to power of Hitler in 1933, ten years after Mussolini's accession in Italy; the Munich Pact of 1938; the death (probably Stalin's murder) of Sergei Kirov, second-in-command in the Soviet party, and a popular threat to Stalin; opening of the era of the purges; Mussolini's Ethiopian campaign; the Spanish Civil War; the failure of the Russians to reach mutual security arrangements with the West European powers, in the face of the growing Nazi menace, as a result of mutual suspicion, shortsightedness, and the divisive nature of the ideology of Marxism-Leninism. Then came the Nazi-Soviet Pact of August 1939, relieving Hitler's eastern front in preparation for his campaign in the west. After the pact came the German invasion of Poland, Soviet occupation of the eastern half of Poland, and the formal opening of World War II. All of these events provide the background for the Stalin revisions, whether contemplated or actually made, in 1952 and 1953.

The Nazi-Soviet Pact had been prepared during months, even years, of Russian probing in Berlin's direction—all unbeknownst to the Western powers. The West was to learn only after the war that as early as 1936 Soviet representatives had discussed with the German Ambassador to Russia, Schulenberg, and others the possibility of establishing "political foundations" for relations with Nazi Germany. But the British and French had attempted to reach some agreement with Stalin but had failed miserably, as they had in preceding months and years. In the spring of 1939, for example, the London government had instructed its ambassador to the Kremlin to inform the Russians that the British were "now disposed to agree that effective cooperation between the Soviet, French, and British governments against aggression in Europe" might be based on a system of mutual guarantees in general conformity with the principles of the League of Nations, "even at the price of meeting several tough Soviet demands." The British ambassador then proceeded to hand the Soviet Deputy Foreign Minister the text of a draft for a treaty between East and West. As one historian of this period, the former Polish diplomat Jan Librach, has observed: "Had the Soviet negotiators really been eager to form [an East-West] front against Hitler, they would have had it then and there." (Soviet histories have totally distorted this period, maintaining, quite without foundation, that the West made no efforts to reach an agreement with Moscow and ignoring the determined Soviet effort throughout the spring and summer of 1939 to strike a deal with the Germans.) After fruitless talks in Moscow between Western envoys and Molotov, the new Foreign Minister, the British ambassador wrote: "I am sorry to say that quite palpably my words produced not the slightest effect; they seemed not to be heard or understood."

When the era of collaboration with Nazi Germany opened, the Communist International was instructed to change its line on German and Italian fascism. Henceforth, said Moscow's instruction to the Comintern, the Nazi war effort would be described as "defensive," the Western Allies as "Anglo-French warmongers." Then followed acts of Communist-inspired sabotage committed in armaments factories throughout the West, including the United States. The Communist party of the United States, until today one of the more loyal Soviet international "detachments," bitterly protested lend-lease aid to Britain in its publications and pamphlets distributed in America, and demanded an arms embargo on all supplies going to the combatant democracies fighting Hitler and Mussolini in Europe or North Africa.

With the pact, Stalin anticipated the opening of a useful and protracted period of cooperation with Germany. This actually occurred, with the Russians supplying the Nazi economy and war machine with vitally needed raw materials—in the first year, totaling 800 million Reichsmarks. These commodities included mineral oil, cotton, iron ore, scrap iron, platinum, manganese, timber, fodder. The Russians assured Berlin that they "had no desire to damage Germany's war economy." As it turned out, they aided and abetted it and planned even greater collaboration, especially with military supplies. Not only trade with Germany, but also mutual bargaining and scheming over broad global spheres of influence took place between 1939 and the Nazi invasion of its friendly partner on June 22, 1941. Meanwhile, Russia invented a pretext for invading Finland (Finland, she alleged, lobbed artillery shells onto Russia in the vicinity of Leningrad), but got bogged down in a war which should have been quickly terminated in Russia's favor, but was not. More reappraisal in the Kremlin, and a strengthened and more professional military command finally saw the defeat of Finland and the signing of a treaty favorable to Russia, in March 1940. Although the Soviet Union was expelled from the Western-led League of Nations because of her winter war against Finland, she had gained some bases to the north, while also availing herself of the time and permission, under the terms of the Nazi-Soviet pact and its secret protocols, to occupy Bessarabia and Northern Bukovina (belonging to Rumania) as well as the three Baltic States of Estonia, Latvia, and Lithuania, which were thereupon Sovietized. When Hitler invaded France and finally entered Paris in June 1940, Molotov, the Soviet foreign minister, sent the Germans a congratulatory message.

Operation Barbarossa, Hitler's grandiose scheme for capturing the whole "Heartland" (Russia) of the Eurasian "World Island," forced Stalin into another zigzag, and the "strange alliance" of East and West in World War II was created. Thus opened the four-year period of what Soviet history books, until today, call the period of "coalition" (*koalitsiya*), or loose ties with the Western Allies, for the purpose of "repulsing the Fascist enemies."

Stalin's Post-World War II Policies

After the war, Stalin made a new reappraisal regressing to many of the harsher policies pursued on the home front as well as abroad before the war. He initiated a crackdown in cultural affairs; a hardening of ideology; restored the Third International (disbanded in 1943) in the form of the Cominform; presented the theory of the two hostile camps (of the capitalists opposed to the Socialists); announced a hard-driving five-year plan backed up by the threat of penalties and charges of "counterrevolutionary activity." He also upgraded the importance of police surveillance, terror, and the use of labor camps, both as punishment and as sources of production, for manpower for canal-digging, among other projects. He also began a violent purge against top leaders, but more quietly than before and usually without recourse to show trials (except in the East European satellites).

On the foreign front after World War II, Stalin proceeded to carry out the plans he had formulated in 1934, when he informed the 17th Party Congress:

The war will surely unleash revolution and put in question the very existence of capitalism in a number of countries, as was the case in the first imperialist war [World War I]. . . . Let not the bourgeoisie blame us if on the morrow of the outbreak of such a war they miss certain ones of the governments that are near and dear to them, and who are today happily ruling by the grace of God . . . There is no doubt that a second war against the USSR will lead . . . to a revolution in a number of countries of Europe and of Asia, and to the overthrow of the bourgeois-landowner governments in these countries.

This warning was echoed two years later by one of Stalin's top aides, Andrei A. Zhdanov, who said:

Round us lie small countries which dream of great adventures or allow adventurers to manipulate their territory. We are not afraid of these little countries, but if they do not mind their own business, we shall be compelled to use the Red Army on them.

(Zhdanov, by the way, who is known both for his energetic use of Stalinism against neighboring countries as well as the postwar crackdown on literati in the Soviet Union, was recently honored for his "internationalism" [a euphemism for what the Chinese call "Soviet hegemonism"] in the long 80th anniversary commemoration of his death published in *Pravda,* March 10, 1976. The Zhdanov commemoration was obviously motivated by the continuing Soviet effort to dampen down nationalism within the Soviet bloc [represented by the Yugoslavs and the Rumanians, the latter of whom were victimized by the expanionist policies of Stalin and Zhdanov in 1940 and later] as well as Western Communist "liberalism" and "right-wing revisionism" often condemned by the Cominform and Kremlin leaders.) Thus was created the "Soviet bloc" or Balkan, Central, and East European states with an area of 560,000 square miles and a population of about 100 million. If the population then ruled by the Mao Tse-tung regime, established in 1949, were also added (750 millon), the combined population under Communist control amounted to about one-third of the world's population in 13 countries.

The threat that Stalin posed to the rest of the globe created great, perhaps too great, Western alarm. As a result, the Dulles policy toward the "captive nations" was heralded in 1952 as allegedly one of "rolling back Communism," or at least of partly continuing the Marshall-Acheson policy of "containment of Communism." The 1952 Republican party program criticized the Democrats' containment policy as being "negative, futile and immoral," but the program also adopted the thesis, which formed part of the theory of containment, that holding the line against Communism would eventually bring the collapse of Communism behind the Iron Curtain in the satellites. And the Republicans went further (from the 1952 program): "The policies we espouse will revive the contagious, liberating influences which are inherent in freedom. They will inevitably set up strains and stresses within the captive world which will make the rulers impotent to continue their monstrous ways and mark the beginning of their end." These words may have alarmed Stalin, his colleagues and his successors, but the leadership that succeeded Stalin was to find out by June 1953, the time of the anti-Communist East German uprisings, that these words were far fiercer than the actual bite of the Republican Administration elected in 1952. The East German revolt was crushed by Soviet tanks and guns, and the United States did not lift a finger, nor did it in the uprisings to follow, in Hungary and Poland (1956), and during the Dubcek crisis in Czechoslovakia in 1968 and the workers' riots in Poland in 1970 and 1976.

For a time, it looked as though Stalin was intent upon Sovietizing other Balkan countries (Greece and Turkey, for example), to say nothing of Western Europe. But no one in the West knew then, or knows today, whether Stalin actually entertained such grandiose plans toward the West, at least for the immediate future. Few, however, would deny that the dictator was capable of such designs, given the texts of the conversations and secret protocols emanating from the Soviet discussions with the Nazis in 1940, and other documentation. Stalin's thrusting, either with the Red Army, Communist guerrillas, or fifth columns, provoked a reaction, some say "overreaction," in Western quarters, and especially in the United States. In fact, America became cast in the role of defender of Western democracy, analogous to the role it had played during the war as the "arsenal of democracy." With Europe in a weakened state (the opening of the "second crisis" of capitalism), a strong American presence in European affairs was predictable, perhaps natural.

Mutual suspicions between East and West grew apace throughout the immediate postwar period. Contributing to this was Stalin's reiteration of his old 1924 "vow" to the memory of Lenin to protect and to spread Communism. This vow was updated, in case anyone doubted its currency, by confirming statements made right after the war by foreign Communist leaders such as Jacques Duclos of France. It was especially echoed in the famous "Warsaw speech" by Andrei Zhdanov upon the foundation of the Cominform in 1947, when the Soviet Party Secretary expostulated upon the two hostile camps and their irreconcilability, the line developed by Stalin earlier, on February 9, 1946, in his famous electoral address. Soviet imperial rule of its satellites, coupled to reckless thrusts in the direction of Berlin and elsewhere, created a dangerous situation in the heart of Europe. Germany was made the center of tensions between East and West, as this country remained split and frustrated by the great power schism. Crises, like that around Berlin in 1948, continually threatened to ignite World War III. If this were not enough to keep nerves on edge, a colossal "revolutionary" adventure was hatched in the Kremlin: the Korean War.

Mao stayed in the Kremlin in the winter of 1950, and with Stalin and their North Korean allies, worked out plans for boldly crossing the 38th Parallel. Expecting, apparently, little response from the Americans (who had earlier hinted that Korea fell outside their Pacific defense perimeter) and from the Europeans, the Soviet and the Chinese expected to cooperate successfully in the first major postwar effort to forcibly export Communism. (Until today, official Communist materials have at no time admitted to Communist initiation of this war.) The war seesawed back and forth and finally ended in a truce in 1952, which placed forces in a position of confronting each other at the same parallel. Some said the war had been a stalemate, others that the United Nations forces had established an important precedent: Communist expansion by forcible means would not be permitted.

Whatever the truer evaluation of the war's outcome might have been, relations between the East and West sharply worsened as the result of it. At the same time, American public opinion grew increasingly impatient with continued American participation in the far-off war.

Stalin's Last Revisions

It was in 1952 that Stalin began another of his famous reappraisals—in this case, his last. Some of the elements of this last revision figured in the policies that were developed immediately after his death, some of which are still in force today. The outline of new tactics and strategy Stalin developed during his last months as ruler of Russia were in response to the Communist Korean failure, which it surely was (admitted by Khrushchev in his memoirs); the potentiality for a major upturn in Soviet military strength as the new era of modernization with "ultimate weapons" opened; promising developments for the Soviets in the Near East and in South and Southeast Asia; Stalin's belief that a period of rivalry and tension amongst the Allies lay ahead which invited possibilities for adroit Soviet diplomatic maneuvering *vis-à-vis* each Western country; Stalin's stated wish for a fresh reevaluation of the relationship with the United States, looking toward summit meetings and arrangements which might eventually lead toward isolation or at least "neutralization" of the United States as the leader of the capitalist world from its European partners—the latter of whom would be invited to turn eastward and think in "pan-European" terms. This policy harmonized with the old Leninist-Stalinist strategy of dividing the capitalist states from each other: "to take advantage of the conflicts between capitalist states"; "to incite one [enemy power] against the other . . . we Communists must use one country against another," as Lenin put it.

In 1952, if not earlier, Stalin was evidently aware of the "complexities," a commonly used word in Soviet materials for a "dialectical" situation full of contradictions, confronting the leaders of the big powers at that time. Above all, he understood both the military as well as political and diplomatic potentialities offered by atomic bombs and the threat of their use. (The Soviet Union broke the monopoly of the United States in 1949 and developed hydrogen bombs in 1954, only two years later than the United States.) In his memoirs, Khrushchev has described Stalin's interest in this program:

> The most urgent military problem facing us after the war was the need to build nuclear weapons. We had to catch up with the Americans, who had been the first to develop atomic bombs and the first to use them in war.... We knew that the reactionary forces of the world, led by the United States, had decided to place all their bets on nuclear weapons. We also knew that the Western imperialists were not one bit squeamish about the means they used to achieve their goal of liquidating Socialism and restoring capitalism [throughout the Soviet Bloc] ... Stalin drew the correct conclusion: he saw that the reactionary forces of the West were mobilizing against us, that they had already accumulated hundreds of atomic bombs, and that the prospect of a military conflict with the United States was all too possible and not at all encouraging for our side.

With such weapons, the whole of the world's civilization could be regarded as threatened by disaster, which was one of the principal warnings in the propaganda of the Soviet-backed 1950 "Stockholm Peace Appeal." But more importantly, war might be viewed as less likely to break out if its universally devastating consequences were borne in mind, or for that matter, even advertised. This could serve the double purpose in diplomacy as well as in Leninist tactics and strategy on the party-international level of labeling and preventing Western big-power actions which might "precipitate" such a war (through diplomatic intercourse as well as the Communist-led world peace movement); permitting any number of Communist actions—in the form of "just" national-liberation struggle or local wars—to take place under the threat and just short of the outbreak of a world war, expecting that the capitalist side would yield in the face of such a threat. Such diplomatic tactical and strategic use of the threat of ultimate weapons would be possible, of course, only if both sides—

especially, the Soviet and the American within the Eastern and Western blocs—possessed an ample supply of such weapons and the latest vehicles for delivering them, and if the world were aware of these arsenals. Rocket development thereby became all important. And Stalin, accordingly, expedited Soviet research and development of missiles, at a pace far outstripping that of the United States. Soviet rocket development was fully consummated only three years after Stalin's death when, in April 1957, the first test shot of a Soviet missile was made (Sputnik I was put into orbit the following October).

Then Stalin held an interview with James Reston of *The New York Times* in December 1952. During this interview Stalin invited President-elect General Dwight D. Eisenhower to participate in a meeting between the United States and the Soviet Union (which would have been the first since the wartime summits). With the invitation, speculation arose that Stalin was about to undertake some new foreign-policy gambit. The text of Stalin's remarks to Reston included the phrase that was to be so common in official Soviet statements after Stalin's death three months later: *oslableniye mezhdunarodnovo napryazheniya,* relaxation of international tension, or détente. Here is the text of the "Christmas interview," published on the front pages of the Soviet press, December 26, 1952:

Answers of J. V. Stalin to Questions Asked by Diplomatic Correspondent of The New York Times, *James Reston Received on December 21, 1952*

Question: As the moment of the New Year approaches and a new administration takes office in the United States, do you still hold the conviction that the Soviet Union and the United States may live in peace in the coming years?

Answer: I continue to believe that war between the United States and the Soviet Union cannot possibly be considered as inevitable, and that our countries may as before live in peace.

Question: Where, in your opinion, lie the sources of today's international tension?

Answer: Wherever there appears aggressive activities of the policy of "cold war" waged against the Soviet Union.

Question: Do you welcome diplomatic negotiations with representatives of the new Eisenhower Administration for assessing the possibilities of holding a meeting between you and General Eisenhower on the question of relaxation of international tension?

Answer: I regard this proposal favorably.

Question: Will you cooperate in some new diplomatic endeavor for ending the war in Korea?

Answer: I agree to cooperate since the USSR is interested in liquidating the war in Korea.

Stalin customarily chose the questions he wished addressed to him, and in any case, closely edited them for publication. It is clear from the above that he had an important message to convey to Eisenhower, an overture which reflected policy reconsiderations in the Kremlin toward the United States and possibly toward the West generally.

Likewise, Stalin tried to approach the French and the British. This was done in the usual subtle Stalin manner, with a *Pravda* editorial here or a hint there. The French journalist, Georges Bortoli, recalls in his book, *The Death of Stalin* (1975), how Stalin made these gestures. For example, when Stalin received the newly appointed French ambassador, Louis Joxe, in August 1952, the Soviet leader went out of his way and broke a long standing precedent to accord M. Joxe a special audience in the Kremlin. "If NATO is [like] Monsieur the Ambassador says [it is], why don't we join it?" Stalin asked ironically, as his Foreign Minister, Andrei Vyshinsky, looked on dumbfoundedly. Thereupon Stalin inquired abruptly about General de Gaulle, who had been out of office in France for more than six years (but who was invited to make a second visit to the Soviet Union after he returned to power in 1958). As Soviet newspapers prominently advertised the unusual meeting between Stalin and Joxe, the Western press speculated that the Pinay Government in Paris might be in the process of "doublecrossing its Western Allies." After all, it was pointed out, Stalin had never received the British or American ambassadors during the whole postwar period. Actually, Pinay was not doublecrossing the Allies, but "Stalin knew that France was fearful and divided over German rearmament and the European Defense Community," writes Bortoli. And Stalin's heirs were to exploit this fear and thus continue Stalin's tactic after the dictator's death. Stalin, and later on, his successors, clearly sensed this fear and saw it as an opening in France for Soviet diplomatic penetration. A wedge between France and the West was formed in 1955 and was opened wider after 1966 when de Gaulle visited Russia. And it was maintained during the years of "Franco-Soviet cooperation" under Brezhnev in Moscow and Pompidou and Giscard in Paris.

As if to indicate that he wanted to make new moves toward both France and Britain, Stalin posted top diplomats to his embassies in Paris and London in 1952 (for example, Andrei Gromyko in London). Other Stalinite gestures which surely indicated renewed interest in establishing relations with the West included Soviet participation for the first time in the West in the Olympic games (1952) and more numerous peace appeals (from 1951 on) directed at the West. Also, early in 1952 the party changed the party line in an relations with the West—editorial comment in *Pravda*. It was announced that "two kinds of imperialists" exist in the West: "extreme imperialists" and "reasonable imperialists." Western analysts have customarily regarded the late post-Stalin period as the time of the first appearance of the line on "two types of imperialists," but this is not accurate. Moreover, it is possible that de Gaulle, Eisenhower, and Churchill were regarded by Stalin as representatives of imperialist "reasonableness." Churchill's return to power in Britain in 1951 may have suggested to Stalin the possibility of a new round of summits among the big powers never before held in peace time. Stalin's novel inquiries about de Gaulle (in 1952) suggest this possibility, while Soviet press coverage of Churchill's reiterated remarks from 1950 through 1952 favoring summitry between East and West is also a case in point. One of the first of Churchill's proposals was made in March 1950, when the former wartime leader said: "I cannot help coming back to this idea of another talk with Soviet Russia upon the highest level. The idea appeals to me of a supreme effort to bridge the gulf between the two worlds so that each can live their life, if not in friendship, at least without the hatreds of war." Whether Churchill's idea attracted Stalin's attention or suggested an updated, peacetime form of the World War II summits is a matter of conjecture.

Incidentally, it is interesting to see how Soviet leaders, going back to Lenin, tend to regard conservatives, as opposed to Social Democrats, United States Democrats, or British Labourites, as bourgeois opponents with whom they can deal more profitably than liberals. *Commentary* magazine editor, Norman Podhoretz, uttered a long-standing truism when he wrote:

> But the truth is that conservatives in office and practice have been rather less bellicose than their standard rhetorical gestures would lead one to suppose. John Foster Dulles encouraged the idea that the United States would work for the liberation of Eastern Europe from Communist rule, but the Eisenhower administration did nothing. After Richard Nixon took over the conduct of the [Vietnam] war, he sent troops to Laos and Cambodia and bombers to Hanoi, but he also withdrew all American forces from that part of the world, inaugurated a policy of detente with the Soviet Union, and opened up relations with Communist China. Gerald Ford ... went to Helsinki to sign a declaration [1975] legitimating Soviet control of Eastern Europe without even insisting on a reasonable quid pro quo, refused to meet Aleksandr Solzhenitsyn for fear of offending the Soviet Union, and continued the Nixon policy of supplying the Soviets with grain and technology in exchange for little more than a smile from Leonid Brezhnev.

Podhoretz explained that Democratic administrations, by contrast, "went into Korea ... [and] went to war to prevent the fall of South Vietnam." Lenin, Stalin, and Khrushchev, in contrast, showed in their writings and memoirs (Khrushchev was the only one of the three to write memoirs) that they were capable of singling out American or other "bourgeois" leaders, not on the basis of party affiliation alone, but as individual characters. At several places in his memoirs, Khrushchev speaks of the close "study" made of various Presidents of the United States by his agents in order to determine the set of their minds. Khrushchev found Eisenhower to be weak, Kennedy strong; he regarded Nixon and the two Dullesses, John Foster and Allen, to be untrustworthy; he found Adlai Stevenson and Anthony Eden to be reasonable, and Truman hateful. Podhoretz's classification of Republican and Democratic administrations into "soft" and "hard" respectively may have some basis in fact in the history of relations between the United States and the Soviet Union. It is perhaps not entirely true to infer from this that the Kremlin itself adheres to this classification when it deals with administrations in the United States. It probably prefers, instead, to size up each American or Western political leader individually, *personally*, too, if possible.

When Stalin's heir apparent, Georgi Malenkov, addressed the 19th Party Congress in October 1952, he put uncommon stress on national-liberation struggle in the international segment of his report. Here again, Stalin, through Malenkov, seemed to show that he had some new departures from former foreign policy in mind. Was he perhaps impressed by the fast-rising wave of worldwide national-independence movements and decolonization sweeping across the Third World during 1952, and in the period immediately preceding it? Was the Suez Canal an important factor attracting the Soviet leadership's attention in 1952, the year in which the Egyptian independence movement was cresting? That other major factor in Near Eastern politics and geopolitics, oil—a commodity whose industrial and military importance was increasing by leaps and bounds during the postwar period—was that also on Stalin's mind? By 1952, 85 percent of Europe's petroleum imports came from the Middle East. One recalls Molotov's talks in Berlin in 1940 when a Soviet sphere of influence in the oil-rich Near East was one of Stalin's strongest demands in the bargaining with Nazi Germany then taking place. Moreover, a new Soviet look at Iran was overdue, a country into which the Soviets had again attempted to expand immediately after World War II but had been stopped by joint British and American action. They felt that a reevaluation of the tactical line toward Iran was especially timely by 1952, given the growing strength of the pro-Communist Persian Tudeh party and the rise of Mohammed Mossadegh, whose program demanded the nationalization of Western oil concerns in Iran, a precedent worth encouraging, from the Kremlin's point of view. The manner in which Stalin's anti-Jewish campaign—the "Jewish Doctors' Plot"—of the first weeks of 1953 was advertised throughout the Arab world also seemed tied in with the increasingly anti-Israeli posture of the Soviet Union and the evident sudden rise in importance for Soviet foreign policy of the Near Eastern Arab component. Diplomatic relations with Israel were broken in February 1953. Accordingly, Bortoli wrote: "By carrying the anti-Semitic campaign to its highest pitch, after having whipped it up for many months in all the Socialist countries, the Soviet proved that it had, without the slighest hesitation, now ranged itself on the Arab side." The case of the Jewish doctors, he maintains, "was obviously part of a foreign policy maneuver." In his concluding remarks at the 19th Party Congress, Stalin strongly advised the foreign Communist parties' "shock brigades" to raise high the "banner of national independence." And in Stalin's last ten days, there were indications from the Kremlin of a "Stalin Plan" for the Third World.

The trade minister Anastas Mikoyan's speech to the congress contained some hints of new policies and priorities on the foreign front. While the Soviet satellite bloc trade would, of course, continue to dominate the Soviet trade picture to the tune of 80 percent of all its 1952 commerce, Mikoyan nevertheless talked of offering "unselfish" assistance to underdeveloped countries. This anticipated a number of trade deals soon to be made by the leadership that had followed Stalin with such key countries as Iran, Afghanistan, and India. Presaged by Mikoyan was that new arrival on the foreign scene of the mid-fifties of "Soviet foreign aid," which never came near to replacing the aid offered by the United States and to a lesser extent, that of other Western nations. But it became an important factor nonetheless at the end of the regime of Stalin and after which was used to nibble away at the "rear" fringes of the "imperialist world" and to give a realistic foundation to the Soviet claim that the Soviet Union was the "true friend" of independence movements, former colonial nations, and the Third World as a whole on the three-A continents. Between 1954 and 1956, these countries were actually singled out for Soviet largesse: Afghanistan, India, Burma, Egypt, Syria, Indonesia, Cambodia, Communist China and Pakistan, aid totaling over $1 billion.

The German question was another of the perennial problems facing Stalin and his successors throughout the postwar period, indeed perhaps the most important single European problem. Soviet policy toward Germany was aimed at keeping this potentially strong and dangerous country weak, or at least, safely partitioned and the more industrialized western half of the country from rearming or becoming a fully empowered participant in the Western defense system. Toward the end of Stalin's life, a major phase in Soviet-German policy was reaching a climax: the all-out effort to prevent Germany's entrance, even partially, into NATO. Since 1948 and the Berlin blockade, the West German economy had become one of the healthiest of the Western economies. Her shipbuilding industry was the second largest in the world; she was far exceeding the production level attained at the time of Hitler's Third Reich, which was geographically larger than the Federal Republic of Germany; and she ranked fourth in industrial power behind America, Russia, and Britain. The issues of former territories, German reunification, and West German participation in NATO (which was formalized in October 1954) thus sharpened proportionately as West German power grew. On top of this, West Germany (officially established only in 1955) was led by the stubbornly pro-Western conservative, Konrad Adenauer, who was certainly no friend of the Soviet Union. Furthermore, the incoming Eisenhower Administration in the United States was bent upon urging its West European partners into greater responsibility for their own national defense, and for contributions to NATO. The new American mood, which Stalin and his successors seemed to sense, was one of neo-isolationism. Thus, an era of some independent action on the part of European states, outside of American guidance, and perhaps including defense decisions which might or more likely might not contribute to the integrity or future of NATO seemed to be opening in 1952 and 1953. This represented for the Soviet Union both opportunities as well as dangers, since an independently acting Germany was at the same time a more unpredictable

Germany than the one that had emerged vanquished from World War II. "The pattern of a new Europe, capable of standing on its own feet," observed an American historian of diplomacy, "definitely began to emerge [in the early 1950s]."

On the domestic front, too, Stalin toyed with some new policies, some of which were traditionally "hard," others suggestive of new changes. Some of these were revealed in the dictator's last writing, *Economic Problems of Socialism in the USSR* (1952). One of the theoretic positions and long-term economic goals outlined in the writing was gradually, not precipitously, to merge the two types of land-usage systems, the collective farm and state farm. This policy was continued under Stalin's successors with the gradual and large-scale mergers, the establishment of state farms, executed under Khrushchev, and particularly in Kazakhstan after 1954 where Leonid Brezhnev eventually played an important role in these mergers. Stalin also began to anticipate the future communist society, which was picked up by his successors when the new party program was finally adopted, after years of discussion, in 1961 under Khrushchev's leadership. Stalin had also anticipated measures to bring about the "withering away of the state," or as interpreted at the time as well as after his death, for upgrading the importance of "public" organizations compared to strictly governmental institutions. Here, too, Khrushchev seemed to be under the influence of Stalin's last instructions when he had written into the 1961 party program precisely this emphasis, in the society to come, upon "social organizations," some of which were already being formed under Khrushchev's leadership (such as the public militia, and the boarding schools, both of which were construed as proto-communist institutions). Also, many Western observers detected a rather unusual stress laid upon light industry in the reports made in 19th Party Congress in October 1952. Still, under the new five-year plan for 1951 to 1955, heavy industry was to get, as usual, the bulk of the investments. Defense expenditures also were increased, but they were more conscientiously concealed than earlier in the published statistics, as though to enhance the subtle emphasis being placed upon consumer goods. Eventually, consumer goods minister Alexei Kosygin delivered a speech to the congress that was uncommonly favorable to the production of consumer goods.

In addition to Stalin's hints of new peaceful policies—the

invitation to hold a summit with President Eisenhower, and the gestures toward France, among others—we should consider other policies that Stalin promulgated late in his regime that were strikingly different in purpose. One of the most respected of Western Kremlinologists of the Stalin era, Boris I. Nicolaevsky, was convinced that Stalin harbored a number of plans near the end of his life that pointed toward World War III. And for this reason, Nicolaevsky was quite certain that Stalin had been dispatched by his colleagues who were determined to help usher in a period of relative international calm, at least so far as the Soviet Union was concerned. In this way, they could continue the military modernization program begun under Stalin and develop an imposing arsenal of thermonuclear-tipped rockets and a dominant position in world politics. One thing was obvious, Stalin had some new, bold military policies in mind, Nicolaevsky insisted. This was strongly suggested by his dismissals of General Sergei Shtemenko as Chief of Staff and Lev Mekhlis as chief of the Main Political Administration of the armed forces, both of which occurred in the early weeks of 1953. Marshal V.D. Sokolovsky was appointed in his place, and he was regarded in the West as one of the more hawkish of Soviet military men. At the very least, Sokolovsky was known to be an ardent partisan of Soviet military buildup and modernization of conventional as well as strategic arms. In appointing him Chief of the General Staff, Stalin obviously contemplated some revised military strategy, either in terms of the external use of Soviet armed forces or its radical reorganization at home, or both. Still another important occurrence was the mysterious death of the commander of the élite guard of the Kremlin, Major-General Pyotr Kosynkin. *Izvestia* described his death as "premature," a euphemism for untoward circumstances. Even more significant was the sudden disappearance of Alexander Poskrebyshev, Stalin's closest lieutenant. Whether Stalin himself dispatched this notorious schemer, who so closely resembled Tsar Boris Godunov's adviser, Shuisky, or someone in the Stalin entourage eliminated him, remains another of the many Kremlin enigmas surrounding the events immediately preceding the dictator's death. For Nicolaevsky and others, these occurrences more than documented the existence of suspicious and portentous developments in the inner councils of the Kremlin just on the eve of Stalin's (alleged) stroke, March 1, 1953.

The hypothesis that Stalin was bent upon abrasive if not adventurous policies and a hard line that Nicolaevsky made, was supported by other events that took place throughout Stalin's last 15 months in power. For example, in his interview with Pietro Nenni in July 1952, Stalin indicated that Soviet policy for the next ten to 15 years would consist of sitting out the cold war, and, in fact, keeping international tensions at a high level. In addition, Soviet U.N. delegate Yakov Malik stated, in 1950, that "World War III has already begun." This characterized quite well Stalin's view of world affairs from 1950 to his death. Accordingly, *Economic Problems of Socialism in the USSR* predicted war between the capitalist states, but not necessarily between them and the Soviet Union, a view which is difficult to construe as being one of "peaceful coexistence." Nevertheless, this Leninist-Stalinist expression began to be merged dialectically with the "hard line" in Soviet materials during the same period, between 1949 and 1953.

Hard-line features aside, it seems quite evident that Stalin did hint at flexible policies at the very end of his life which were to be picked up and pursued by his successors.

Although Stalin's successors began to advocate peaceful coexistence with the West, and cooperation between East and West, they also decided to emphasize nationalism, or to encourage nationalistic strivings in colonial and former colonial countries to enhance Soviet revolutionary positions worldwide. To do this they especially decided to concentrate on the imperialist rear in the Middle East and Asia. Socialism was to be achieved in these countries by installing Communist leaders immediately and thereby avoiding the necessity of these countries' having to pass through a painful "bourgeois phase" that would be dependent on capitalist nations.

The new leaders also decided to attempt to fashion with Red China an axis of working relations whereby Chinese troops might be used as proxies to expand Communist influence throughout Asia, as was tried in Korea, and possibly in Africa and Latin America (most recently, Cubans have performed this role).

However, they also wanted to guard against the possibility that

Maoist China might not agree to such a Soviet-led axis, given Mao's notorious jealousy of Stalin and his suspicions of Russian intentions to make thrusts into the periphery around China, especially into India and Southeast Asia.

Aftermath of Stalin's Death

Malenkov made the new policy public that the Soviet Union would follow after Stalin's death in his funeral oration:

> The Soviet Union has followed and will continue to follow a consistent policy of maintaining and strengthening peace; the policy of struggle against the preparations for and unleashing of war; the policy of international cooperation and the development of commercial links with all countries, a policy which stems from the Lenin-Stalin formulation on the possibility of prolonged coexistence and peaceful competition of the two systems, capitalist and socialist.
>
> The people want peace, they hate war.... We will not permit the flowing of blood of millions of people; we will achieve peaceful construction of a happy life. [The main task] is not to permit the outbreak of a new war, and to live in peace with all countries. The Communist party of the Soviet Union and the Soviet Government consider as the most correct, necessary, and just foreign policy to be one of peace between all nations based on mutual trust, an effective policy *based on deeds and supported by deeds....* Any governments are criminal ones if they seek to deceive the peoples by going against this sacred desire to maintain peace and not to permit a bloody slaughter. The Communist Party and the Soviet Government stand by the position that a peace policy between nations is the only correct policy answering the vital interests of all peoples.

Lavrenti Beria, the security chief, keeper of the labor camps, and commander of Soviet subversives abroad, stressed that the principal task now confronting Soviet foreign policy was to preserve peace by *preventing both the preparation and the unleasing of world war.* Like Malenkov, he also addressed an appeal to all capitalist countries for increased trade and mutual understanding. Beria also warned against what he called "plots hatched by enemies of the Soviet state," against which "vigilance must be upgraded."

Molotov let it be known that policies that were only hinted at earlier would now be set rapidly into motion by the leadership that succeeded Stalin. For example, Molotov reminded the broad audience, at home and abroad, that the Soviet Communist party was not only in charge of affairs within the borders of the Soviet Union, but had worldwide responsibilities, *as a party,* as the "leading force throughout the worldwide workers' movement." He praised Stalin for his various adjustments in theory to present international realities, "basing himself on the science of Marxism-Leninism." In foreign policy, said Molotov, the "Soviet state has no aggressive aims whatsoever, but neither will it, on its part, allow any interference in the affairs of other countries." Soviet foreign policy, he said, is a "Stalin one, a peace policy. It is a policy of keeping peace between the peoples, an unwavering policy of keeping and deepening peace as well as waging the struggle against preparations for and the launching of a new war." Molotov appealed to the West for international "cooperation" and commerce, "if those countries wish it, too."

Two paragraphs later in the oration, Molotov brought up the ticklish subject of "national-liberation struggle." This problem has particular significance, he said, "*under present conditions . . .* when in the colonial or dependent countries the national-liberation movement is growing." In the next sentence, Molotov said that the Soviet Union would remain "true to the principles of proletarian internationalism," which was to become a common phrase in the Soviet statements of the 1970s. "Proletarian internationalism" is, of course, a euphemism for Soviet hegemony over the international Communist and pro-Communist movement in the form of a "center," as well as Soviet initiative in the extension of monetary and arms aid to international Communist and fellow-traveling movements and elements. Molotov added that this expression of

Soviet-led internationalism also embraced the "friendly ties to toilers in the capitalist countries." Like Malenkov and Beria before him, Molotov put a gentle but unmistakable stress upon Stalin's reliance upon Lenin and Leninism, in the oft-repeated phrase, which Molotov accentuated with pauses "together with whom. . .", meaning together with Lenin, which he repeated four times in one short paragraph, ending with "Stalin is the great continuer of the work of Lenin."

By December of 1953, eight months after Stalin's death, the name "Stalin Constitution" was changed to "Soviet Constitution," in the commemoration of the adoption of the constitution. Still earlier (in April), the principle of "collective leadership" had been written into party practice with the clear hint that one-man Stalin rule had been arbitrary and constricting. Stalin's successors worked out a system by which the party (headed by Khrushchev) and the government (headed by Malenkov) would be run by means of a separation of powers and a system of checks and balances. As a result, the collectivity of the leadership and the policy differences that existed among the leaders brought a certain ambivalence to the foreign policies that began to surface during the first post-Stalin years.

New Departures

Still, a number of new policies indicated clear departures from what had preceded them, while also indicating that some of the hints detected in Stalin's last months would be carried forward by the successors. Toward China, the team of Malenkov and Khrushchev displayed uncommon friendliness, almost to the extent of condescension. For example, in the first days after Stalin's passing, the Soviet press published a doctored photograph which depicted Malenkov standing triumphantly next to Mao. But the signal could have been taken several ways. The new leaders had certainly singled out China for special attention (the country was listed out of alphabetical order in the funeral orations and had the flattering adjective "great" appended to its formal title), as the photograph of Malenkov and Mao symbolized. Still, the hint in Soviet quarters was obvious that, in the aftermath of Stalin's death, the leadership of the Communist world would not pass exclusively to the more veteran and better known leader, Mao, and his regime. Moreover, by thrusting Malenkov into the foreground so conspicuously, Moscow seemed to be warning China that it would strongly assert itself in the wake of Stalin. The particular references to Vietnam (in Malenkov's address), and to Asia as a whole in the orations, also indicated this.

As I have mentioned above, the Russians decided to try to form an axis with China. Accordingly, the team of Malenkov and Khrushchev began to display a friendliness, almost a condescension, towards the Chinese, and Malenkov and Khrushchev made tangible overtures to China in 1955 by returning a considerable portion of vital and strategic real estate which had been acquired as a result of World War II or earlier. Actually, two prior Sino-Soviet agreements, in 1950 and 1952, had already promised China the return of the Manchurian Chang Chun railway, and the ports and naval bases of Dalny (Dairen) and Port Arthur (Liushun) to the People's Republic. In addition to these "generous" actions, later repented by the Soviets when the Sino-Soviet cold war began in 1958, the Soviets agreed to disband the notorious "joint-stock companies," which had been run mostly by Russians in the strategic western area of Sinkiang and the northern industrial region of Manchuria. These concessions followed delicate summit meetings between the new Moscow leadership and Mao and his top leaders in 1954, meetings that were more uneven than harmonious, according to Khrushchev's memoirs and other sources of information. According to Mao, for example, other territorial questions were put to the Russians by the Chinese at the 1954 summit, "but [the Russians] refused to talk to us." The outcome of the first meetings of the Russians and Chinese after Stalin died and the overall relationship were problematical, at best. After 1958, the relationship steadily soured.

Stalin's successors were bent upon rapidly undoing and erasing a number of Stalin's harsher methods, to gain worldwide respectability. At the United Nations, the Soviets turned on a conciliatory attitude, at long last accepting the appointment of Trygve Lie as Secretary-General, which they had strongly opposed under Stalin. Moreover, Yugoslavia was approached almost hours after the installation of the Malenkov regime, although the famous "journey to Canossa" of Khrushchev, by way of apologizing for

Stalin's hostility toward the Tito regime, could not be arranged until 1955. Diplomatic relations with Israel were resumed, Molotov indicating that Jerusalem had assured the Soviet Union that it would not take part in any alliances or agreements that had "aggressive aims against the Soviet Union." The policy toward India, as already hinted under Stalin when the late leader busied himself with any number of interviews and consultations with Indians in his last months, was turned even more toward conciliation. The Soviet encylopedia essay on Mahatma Gandhi was totally rewritten so that this "defender of Indian independence" was no longer depicted as a bourgeois-imperialist "lackey." Relations with India greatly improved after 1953. This, of course, was actually another Soviet effort to penetrate the Third World. Other conciliatory moves, which were more than mere gestures, could be listed as important departures from the just-concluded Stalin period: The Soviets renounced their claims to Kars, Ardahan, and Artvin, the Turkish territories that they had demanded ever since 1945. The Soviets also abandoned their demand that sea and air bases in the Turkish Straits area should be jointly controlled by Turkey and Russia. Malenkov indicated that the long-standing Stalin policy of converting Turkey and the Straits into mere satellites of the Soviet Union had been tabled. However, Malenkov indicated that the Montreux Convention of the 1930s, regulating conditions for traffic passing through the Dardanelles and Bosporus in and out of the "Russian lake" of the Black Sea, was still in force. The new regime obviously wanted to indicate that it wished to pursue a more flexible attitude toward world affairs than formerly. And to achieve a "relaxation of tension" with Europe, America, and the world at large. The Ministry of Foreign Affairs was entirely overhauled, enlarged, and streamlined to prepare for these new global policies.

Tensions, however, were not relaxed, for Indochina caused conflict between East and West. Moreover, part of Peking's strategy during and after the Korean conflict had been to extend its influence in areas in Asia bordering on the People's Republic of China. Tibet was one of these areas, but so also was Vietnam. With the defeat of the French at Dienbienphu by the Communist-led Vietminh in May 1954, the entire Communist bloc, but in particular Peking, saw a golden opportunity to win for the

Communists all of South Vietnam, Laos, and Cambodia, which they had wanted ever since the days of the Comintern (in which Ho Chi Minh was an active participant). At the Geneva Conference of 1954 the Communists hoped that the peace they negotiated with the French would leave non-Communist South Vietnam defenseless and internally weak. They hoped that this would become an area which could not achieve internal stability or enough external defensive strength to ward off Communism from the north. However, increasing American support, from material aid under the Eisenhower Administration (between 1953 and 1959) to outright military support in the form of troops under the Kennedy and Johnson Administrations, delayed the long-standing Communist program of spreading the Communist system throughout Southeast Asia. A further complication, which arose after 1960, was the Sino-Soviet conflict. This Far Eastern cold war tended more to step up both Soviet and Chinese involvement in Vietnam than to deflate it and to encourage confrontation with the United States. Both powers appeared to be competing for the loyalty of North Vietnam, under Ho Chi Minh's leadership, which was bent upon forcible unification of the whole country, and possibly North Vietnamese domination over all of Southeast Asia. But they also seemed to relish the chance to challenge the United States as well, for the increasingly deepening involvement of the United States in the war—with the military restrictions which the political aspects of the war imposed upon the American military arsenal of thermonuclear weapons—invited the prospects of putting the United States into what the Soviets called a dilemma. The Communists also reasoned that the involvement of the United States in the war would encourage the West European powers to dissociate themselves from America's Vietnam enterprise in particular and its foreign policy in other respects as well. This suited the overall Soviet strategy of dividing the West and isolating the United States from the European members of NATO. Of course, these negative consequences of the Vietnam war had long since occurred to a number of the war's critics in the United States, especially those (both civilian and military) who put America's basic national interest above the particular programs and posturings of the "Radical Left" (among them, Hans J. Morgenthau and Henry A. Kissinger).

The new Kremlin team also realized that the tight reins held on the East European bloc would have to be loosened if these nations ever were to cooperate with Moscow. The Russian leaders concluded that they could no longer resort to the fear and terror evoked by Stalin and his methods because East European Communist leaders had begun to assert themselves, to pressure for more independence in formulating national policies, although they never questioned basic Soviet tactics and strategy, the "General Line," in foreign policy. Permission to experiment in the domestic area was granted by Moscow, and a sentiment of "centrifrugality" immediately swept over the Soviet empire. In Hungary, some decollectivization of agriculture was permitted, and a degree of private management of small industry. But decollectivization predictably became popular with Hungarian peasants and eventually had to be restricted. In East Germany, various types of relaxation helped prepare conditions for the upsetting riots in East Berlin of June 1953, ignited by attempted price hikes following the brief period of relaxation and relative availability of consumer goods. To greater or lesser degrees, "liberalization" measures were carried out as satellite leaders took advantage of their newly gained leverage by promoting the "New Course" or the notion of "many roads to Socialism." As to Yugoslavia, the apologetic "journey to Canossa" was executed by Khrushchev in May 1955 to relax the bitterness and tensions of the Stalin years. This vacuum that existed after Stalin died, combined with Moscow's relative permissiveness, was to have important consequences for all the aspects of the relations between East and West, not to mention Soviet foreign policy as a whole.

On the domestic front, the Soviet leaders continued the policy of relaxing the harsher features of Stalinism. For example, amnesties were announced affecting the release of some political prisoners. Another highly symbolic departure, during the 1953 "thaw," was the successors' decision to open the grounds of the Kremlin to Soviet citizens as well as to foreign visitors. Undoubtedly, reasoned the new regime, this gesture would abet the process by which the notorious "Kremlin Wall" would cease to appear totally impenetrable and forbidding. The partial thaw also extended to culture and letters. Such well-known figures as Ilya

Ehrenburg and Dmitri Shostakovich began to speak out, although very hesitantly and tentatively, against excessive controls over the arts. The new leadership committed itself to a policy of candor about agriculture. In September 1953, First Secretary Khrushchev frankly described to the party Central Committee the deplorable state of Soviet agriculture. He pointed out that per capita consumption of food had not improved over that of the 1913 figure. Following this, it was hinted that Stalinite collectivization had been too brutal, although no Soviet official in the time after Stalin was gone has ever suggested that an alternative to collectivization ever existed or could exist in the Soviet Union. In his "inaugural address" of August 1953, Premier Malenkov strongly indicated that consumer-goods production would be given more attention than it had been formerly.

A third crucial area of Soviet policy, East-West relations, also underwent refurbishment under the new leadership of the Kremlin, although some basic theories of Stalin and Lenin acted as strong influences, as well as what appears to be Stalin's own thinking in his last months. For in the opening years of the post-Stalin period, Soviet policy showed definite signs of seeking some form of accommodation with the West. The most timely development was the rapid solution of the problems surrounding the formal end of hostilities in Korea. Reston's interview with Stalin in December 1952 had contained the strong hint that a summit meeting between Stalin and Eisenhower (possibly in Moscow or Washington) could have solved the Korean problem. But Stalin's successors moved quickly and confidently to do this. The truce agreement was combined with a renewed Sino-Soviet bid to seat Communist China (which also sought "respectability") within the United Nations. Some observers were skeptical then, many more certainly were by 1960, that the Soviets were sincere in these efforts to seat Red China, even back in the years when China and Russia were friendly, between 1950 and 1953. But both powers, China and Russia, may have reasoned that "normalization" of relations between East and West and the new policy of the relaxation of tensions also between East and West, combined with pursuit of a number of basic Communist global designs, would be expedited by China's joining the United Nations. Both the People's Republic of China and the Soviet Union made a good deal of the fact that membership in the United Nations was rapidly shifting, in the numbers of countries represented within the General Assembly, to a preponderance of "three-A" nations. From 1955 to 1965, for example, 35 new Asian and African nations were added to the roster of the United Nations, including Tunisia (1956), Morocco (1956), Ghana (1957), Malaya (1957), Guinea (1958). Altogether, the whole Asian-African complex of nations comprised 1.7 billion people in 1965. However, from the time of the Bandung Conference (1955), Communist China never recognized the Soviet Union as a true component of this world, although two-thirds of Russia lies in Asia. This "colored-people's" policy of the leaders in Peking was to have enormous importance for Soviet relations with the West, and with the United States in particular, in the years to come.

4

Détente-I: 1955 to the Fall of Khrushchev

During the last months of Stalin's reign, the Russians seriously considered forming an accommodation with the West. However, as we have seen, they still hoped to divide the countries of the West without having to invade territory outright. Also, we have seen how the Soviets wanted peace in order to strengthen their economy and defenses. The nations of the West also wanted to establish peace if only because the notion of "rolling back Communism" had become obsolete.

The Soviets also wished to encourage a respectability for themselves, in order, actually, that they might gain objectives that they had wanted since the time of Lenin. They hoped that the United States would accept the status quo in Eastern Europe in the effort to maintain peace (which the United States did in effect by signing the Helsinki agreement of 1975). The Russians hoped to reduce fears of "Stalinist Russia" (now no longer Stalinist as the leadership wished to underline) and bring about withdrawal of American forces from Europe. They also hoped to neutralize Germany as Austria had been or prolong four-power occupation.

As we have said, the Russians advocated peace in order to gain time to improve the Soviet economy and strengthen their armed forces. But they also hoped that by advocating peace the Western nations could be induced to decelerate their own military programs and give the Soviets the chance to catch up with the West. And, the policy of peaceful coexistence and relaxation of tension would also give the Russians the chance to strengthen the Warsaw Pact nations with conventional weapons until Soviet armed strength was sufficient for the Russians themselves to "hold the line" in Europe. Finally, the Russians wanted to establish peaceful relations with the West so that they could concentrate on offsetting China's growing influence and prestige in the East following the Korean War and resulting from its strong backing of "national-liberation" throughout the Afro-Asian world after 1953 and the Bandung Conference of 1955.

During 1954 and 1955, the concessionary Soviet mood toward the West, and toward the United States as the West's leader, began to assume what Malenkov had promised in his March 9 funeral oration—a peace policy "backed by deeds." The Soviets evidently wished to indicate strongly that relaxation of tension should begin above all with the most powerful capitalist states. As mentioned earlier, this démarche seemed to serve a number of larger demands of Soviet grand strategy. First, if Stalin was correct that the foreseeable future would more likely witness tension among capitalist countries rather than discord between East and West, then it was logical to cultivate relations with each Western capitalist nation separately. This would accord with the old Leninist and Cominternist strategy of egging on the imperialists into mutually debilitating struggle, perhaps even war. Lenin's strategy was embodied in the following declaration to the Comintern in 1928 and has been repeated in Soviet materials since:

> [The peace policy] provides the best basis for taking advantage of the antagonisms existing between the imperialist states. The aim of this policy is to guard the international revolution and to protect the work of building up Socialism— the progress of which revolutionizes the world. It strives to postpone for as long as possible the conflict with imperialism.

As to the motivation for adopting a concessionary posture toward the West as it related to military concerns, Stalin and his successors obviously anticipated an emerging period of Soviet military modernization and buildup, a process that actually had been started under Stalin. The Soviets had been working feverishly on the development of rockets since 1945, with the help of Nazi V-1 and V-2 specialists captured at the end of World War II. A breakthrough could be expected in the next few years. Once these rockets were developed and put into production, the Soviets strategic-weapon component would be given a sizable boost. (Their strategic air force was growing, too, including Myasishchev M-4 "Bisons" and Tupolev-16 "Badgers," heavy and medium jet bombers and Tupolev-95 "Bears.") But a period of relative international calm was necessary for this modernization and buildup to take place. Relaxation of tension well suited this military purpose, especially if it "softened up" NATO by doing what Malenkov had indicated so significantly in his August 1953 inaugural address:

If today, under conditions of tension in relations, the North Atlantic bloc is rent by internal strife and contradictions, the lessening of this tension may lead to its disintegration.

Moreover, the Western powers should be relieved of alarm, to an extent, over Soviet activities in the field of armaments in order to prevent them from embarking on the same program. This would in turn serve the purpose of diplomatically splitting off the European allies from America—a cardinal Stalin policy goal. In order to proceed quietly with their armaments program, the Soviets felt that two measures were necessary: concealing expenditures for defense and research and development in the published state budget and showing a concessionary attitude toward the West. The peace policy "based on deeds" toward Western disarmament proposals obviously would be not followed by any intention of carrying out effective disarmament. On the disarmament question, the Soviet began to indicate in 1954 that they, too, now favored step-by-step disarmament, according to the plan of the United States. They hinted that they might even be willing to yield on such issues as international inspection and curbing the arms race by leveling off production of certain types of weapons.

But it soon became apparent that Moscow was advancing

proposals for peace that would only help the Russians. "Moscow persisted in advancing proposals that would benefit only one side militarily," reported a team of M. I. T. armaments experts in the mid-1960s, as they looked back to the preceding decade of the first détente. For example, the Soviets insisted, onesidedly, that the United States close down its vital overseas bases, and it demanded the exclusion of certain types of military "objects of control" and inspection, thereby vitiating the effectiveness of enforced disarmament. In all its calls for peace, Moscow banked on gaining the support of the moderate political forces. These forces hopefully would apply pressure on their governments to accept the Soviet conditions for peace and thereby provide the conditions under which the Soviets could build up their military strength covertly.

The "Spirit of Geneva," 1955

The Soviets decided to advance their goals by calling for a summit to be attended by Britain, France, the United States, and the Soviet Union. The February 1954 Berlin conference of the foreign ministers of East and West was the important forerunner of the summit. The communiqué from this meeting spoke of the "better understanding" of the international situation resulting from the conference (Pravda, February 20, 1954). The meeting in Geneva in July 1955 was to work toward pan-European conciliation, including especially agreement over the future of the divided country of Germany. Disarmament, too, was on the agenda, as was discussion of the possible inspection and control over atomic energy and atomic weapons. But these issues were only of superficial importance to the Russians at this stage of the game. They really wanted to bring about an agreement whereby the American withdrawal from Europe could be expedited. The American presence in Europe retarded Soviet influence in the area, possibly outright Soviet expansion.

Germany especially was to be considered, for NATO, an institution largely sponsored and supported by the United States, had already admitted West Germany on a restricted basis. Communist parties in France as well as other NATO countries had made considerable headway in alarming the population, or at least drawing their attention to the danger which German rearmament represented, partial though the rearmament was. Moreover, NATO was depicted as needlessly expensive, an American toy fast becoming obsolete as the reputed Soviet danger diminished into the appearance of a phantom kept alive merely by the Communist-baiting Americans and "their" cold war. Thus, at Geneva, the Soviet representatives—Bulganin, Khrushchev, Molotov, and the decorous Marshal Zhukov—"generously" offered German unification on the neutralized Austrian model, a totally disarmed Germany overseen by the four victorious wartime partners (including the Soviet Union).

The Russians also proposed at this time a stage-by-stage dismantling of NATO and the Warsaw Pact alliance, formed in 1955 just months before the Geneva Conference (the alliance, however, had existed in a nonlegal, covert form at least since 1950). Bulganin asserted with almost comical deceptiveness that, "Our objective should be to have no foreign troops remaining on the territories of Europe." No one, outside the narrow bloc of Communists and their supporters, could have possibly believed in the sincerity of such Soviet overtures, given the urgent need for Soviet troops of occupation for internal security in the satellite countries, especially in an era of anti-Communist uprisings (such as the violent clashes in East Germany and elsewhere in June 1953). The West, moreover, was totally suspicious of Soviet calls for a reunited Germany for two reasons: first, based on past experience throughout Central and Eastern Europe, political reunification, or an all-German government, would amount to Soviet domination through the single ruling Communist party in such a government; considering a united Germany's potential power, this would represent a colossal and intolerable disturbance of the power equilibrium in Europe; second, Stalin and his successors had, in any case, given no indication that they had changed their minds on the danger that a reunited Germany represented to the Soviet Union: the Soviets had always favored their own version of the "Morgenthau Plan" advanced by the United States or of England's Lord Vansittart by which Germany would remain permanently enfeebled.

These and other Soviet proposals presented at Geneva were always proffered amidst an uncommon show (for Soviet negotiators) of joviality and friendly banter. Geneva, in short, was a charade to help divide the West by reducing tension; to build military strength at home; and to aid in the process by which colonial and ex-colonial countries in the Third World, the "Zone of Peace," could be detached from the West as sources of raw materials or markets for Western goods.

The 20th Party Congress, 1956

The Russians persisted in their efforts to "achieve peace," but to divide and overwhelm the West. At the 20th Party Congress held in 1956, Khrushchev did, indeed, attack Stalin, but it is too often overlooked that the old foreign policy was left intact, that it was once again given a solid, Communist-internationalist underpinning. Khrushchev had no criticism of the basic Stalinist tactics and strategy; his efforts at de-Stalinization were made mostly to embarrass his rivals and were unrelated to foreign policy (with the notable exception of the Yugoslav case, where, said Khrushchev, Stalin had erred). Moreover, no attempt was made to separate peaceful coexistence from the rest of the Stalinist heritage. Finally, Khrushchev hoped to enhance and dramatize his policy, not only by designating it to be doctrinal and no mere pro tem tactic, but by partially updating Lenin's philosophy in the process.

Above all, it was necessary to fit diplomacy aimed at relaxing tensions together with the more fundamental concept of peaceful coexistence into what the Kremlin now described as the "decisive stage" in the victory of Socialism throughout the world. The description of the "present era as the decisive stage," which first appeared in ideological statements in the mid-1950s, has been reiterated at successive Russian Communist party congresses ever since, up to and including the 25th Party Congress held in February and March 1976. Since 1956, the Soviet leaders have apparently seriously believed that the fate of capitalism will be determined during the present period—or in their lifetime—if not by that final clash in arms predicted by Lenin, then by such significant alteration in the equilibrium of forces ("correlation of forces") in the Communist favor that the doom of capitalism will be hastened. This ideological formulation about the fate of capitalism goes by the name of the "General Crisis of Capitalism" (see chart, p. 65). The "law" was said to have been discovered by Lenin, advanced by Stalin, and to remain in force until today (for example, in the greeting to the 1976 Bonn Congress of the West German Communist party). The "crisis" is described as having begun to "sharpen" since the late 1950s because of the spread of "national liberation" and independence throughout the Third World after World War II. The crisis has also sharpened within the capitalist world itself, according to the Communists, since the mid-1950s and they reasserted this at the 20th Party Congress in particular, because of the "militarization of the capitalist economies" in the post-World War II period. This in turn has led to the "increased danger of war." But it has also led to the increased importance of the Soviet contribution to a reversal of the worldwide "correlation of forces" in the Soviet bloc's favor, according to Moscow's calculations, which abets, it claims, the process by which war can be avoided.

Updating Peaceful Coexistence

Khrushchev was careful to point out that he was not entirely revising Lenin's concept of peaceful coexistence, only modernizing it. He argued that Lenin had stipulated (for example, in *Imperialism—the Highest Stage of Capitalism*) that war was "inevitable" as long as capitalism existed anywhere in the world. But the world had changed since Lenin worked out this theory 40 years ago, Khrushchev said. True, capitalism still inevitably contained the seeds of war, which were imbedded in the very nature of capitalism. This could never change, as long as capitalism existed anywhere in the world. What had changed were the noncapitalist world, above all the Soviet-led part of it, and its capacity to deal with the war-ridden danger known as "capitalist imperialism." That is, the correlation of forces was changing in the Socialist favor. The Socialist world was becoming powerful enough to prevent warlike capitalism from being true to its nature. Or putting it another way, said Khrushchev, "war is no longer fatally inevitable." The introduction of the word "fatally" was intriguing, since it clearly did *not* mean that war was not inevitable; only that it was not *fatally* inevitable. And, Khrushchev went on to explain, war cannot be regarded as "fatally" inevitable without entirely vitiating the purpose of a world peace movement. Clearly, if war is completely unpreventable, or destined to occur, any efforts to prevent it are fruitless. Times had changed since Lenin designed his "inevitability" concept, said Khrushchev, in the sense that the Soviet-led world was acquiring the ability to prevent *both the preparation and the launching of war* by the imperialists. The correlation of forces was turning in the Soviet favor—a reflection of the new Soviet missile strength. Moreover, the world peace movement would not only be continued in the forthcoming epoch, but would be activated because war "is not fatally inevitable." It was even possible to form Communist-Socialist fronts within the peace movement. The ideologist Suslov elaborated on the way in which peaceful coexistence and popular-front tactics in capitalist countries might work together:

> Unquestionably, the split of the international workers' movement, when all the forces of the people should be united to fight the menace of a new war, is doubly intolerable. Life has raised a number of important questions on which we have points of agreement with Social Democrats. . . . In today's situation the workers' movement faces such cardinal tasks as defense of peace, national freedom, and democracy. In many capitalist countries the working masses are obviously swinging strongly to the left. The vast majority of rank-and-file members of socialist parties, Christian trade unions, and other organizations favor peace. It is to be assured that the idea of unity will take stronger and stronger hold among the various groups of the working class and lead to practical results. But this will not happen by itself; it will depend largely on us Communists and our efforts in this direction.

As time went on, however, it became apparent to the Russians that it was in Moscow's interest to maintain a *degree of tension,* even to the point of advertising the arms race on *both* sides (rather than abiding by the earlier policy of totally concealing the size of the Soviet side of the arms buildup). This would serve to insert some tension and fear into the European world, where the mightiest arms were located, thus fueling pacifism and the peace movement there and forcing capitalist countries to increase expenditures on arms, with the consequences this was expected to have for inflation and the consequently higher cost of living for the workers. The various Western-Soviet crises early in the Khrushchev era seemed to have been made to order to produce fear in the West.

Khrushchev had some other important modifications to introduce into the "dialectical" concept of peaceful coexistence. Peaceful coexistence sorely needed a doctrinal base, especially in a time when the Russians were relaxing the tensions with the West but stepping up Communist subversion. In close consultation with the party's ideologues (most particularly with Suslov), Khrushchev therefore issued the following statement:

> The Leninist principle of peaceful coexistence of states with differing social systems has always been and remains the General Line of our country's foreign policy.
>
> It has been alleged that the Soviet Union advances the principle of peaceful coexistence merely out of tactical considerations of expediency. Yet, it is common knowledge that we have always, from the very first years of Soviet power, stood with equal firmness for peaceful coexistence. Hence, it is not a tactical move, but a fundamental principle of Soviet foreign policy. . . .
>
> . . . There are only two ways: either peaceful coexistence or the most destructive war in history. There is no third way.
>
> We believe countries with differing social systems can do more than exist side by side. It is necessary to proceed further, to improve relations, strengthen confidence among countries, and cooperate. The historic significance of the famous five principles, advanced by the Chinese People's Republic and the Republic of India and supported by the Bandung Conference and the broad world public, is that in today's circumstance they provide the best form of relations among countries with differing social systems. . . .
>
> Millions of people all over the world are asking whether another war is really inevitable, whether mankind, which has

already experienced two devastating world wars, must endure still a third world war. Marxists must answer this question by taking into consideration the epoch-making changes of the last decade.

As we know, there is a Marxist-Leninist precept that states that wars are inevitable as long as imperialism exists. This thesis was evolved at a time when 1) imperialism was an all-embracing world system and 2) the social and political forces which did not want war were weak, insufficiently organized, and, hence, unable to compel the imperialists to renounce war.

People usually take into account only one aspect of the question: They consider only the economic basis of wars under imperialism. This is not enough. War is not merely an economic phenomenon. Whether there will or will not be a war depends in large measure on the correlation of class and political forces, the degree of organization, and the awareness and resolution of the people. Under certain circumstances, moreover, the struggle being waged by progressive social and political forces can play a decisive role ... Heretofore, the state of affairs was such that the forces opposed to war and that came out against it were poorly organized and lacked the means to oppose their will to the schemes of the war-makers. ...

For that period [of World War I and the eve of World War II], the above-mentioned thesis [on the inevitability of war] was absolutely correct. At the present time, however, the situation has radically changed. Now there is a world camp of Socialism which has become a mighty force. Through this camp, peace forces not only possess the moral but also the material means of preventing aggression. ...

Under these circumstances, of course, the Leninist thesis remains valid: as long as imperialism exists, the economic base giving rise to wars will also remain. That is why we must maintain the greatest vigilance. As long as capitalism survives in the world, reactionary forces ... will continue their drive toward military adventures and aggression, and may try to unleash war. But war is not fatally inevitable. ... The more actively the peoples defend peace, the greater the guarantee that there will be no new war.

Not unexpectedly, Khrushchev's apparent "revision" of Lenin was generally favorably received in the West. This response, however, was premature. In any case, it should have been tempered by the reading of at least two other reports given at the same party congress. In the speech by the chief ideologist, Mikhail Suslov, "correlation of forces," as used by Khrushchev, was spelled out. The forces of peace, said Suslov, alluding to the Socialist bloc countries headed by the Soviet Union, "possess considerable resources for preventing the imperialists from unleashing a war and if they tried to start one anyway, for crushing the aggressors and burying forever both war and the capitalist system." This phrase repeated, almost word for word, a similar explanation Stalin gave in his *Economic of Problems of Socialism in the USSR.*

A second important report that touched on relations with the West, peaceful coexistence, and the prevention of war with capitalist countries was the one given by the foreign minister of that time, Dmitri Shepilov. Shepilov explained that competition with the West was characterized by the inevitable "irreconcilability of the capitalist and Socialist outlooks." The theory that the Russians could establish Socialism in capitalist countries without resorting on war and the fact that the capitalist and Communist outlooks were irreconcilable have remained as theoretic foundations of the present-day Soviet understanding of peaceful coexistence. In the presentations by Khrushchev, Suslov, and Shepilov, Stalinism was merely reworded rather than recast. But Khrushchev had another doctrinal underpinning to give to his updated version of peaceful coexistence: its relation to the tactics and strategy of revolution. Here again, basic Leninism-Stalinism was the salient characteristic. Khrushchev referred to the assertion that Lenin made in 1920 when he stated that "all nations will come to Socialism, that is inevitable, but not all countries will come to Socialism in the same manner; each will introduce its own peculiarity into one or another form of democracy, into one or another variety of the dictatorship of the proletariat." Khrushchev continued by pointing out that the path to Socialism does not inevitably involve civil war, just as earlier he had maintained that world war was not necessary in order to bring down capitalism. In some countries, the First Secretary stated, a "parliamentary road to Socialism" might be followed. But in the strongly capitalist nations—that is, the West European nations and the U.S.—"where capitalism is still strong, where it has in its hands an enormous military and police apparatus, in them the serious opposition shown by reactionary forces is inevitable. There the transition to Socialism will take place under conditions of sharp class and revolutionary struggle." Others have made it clear that whether the revolution in other countries would be peaceful or bloody did not depend on the Communist or pro-Communist forces, but only on the capitalists. In other words, it was explained that if the capitalists opposed or resisted the inevitable march of history, and its standard-bearers, the Communists and their allies, violence would become necessary to overcome capitalist resistance. Or as Suslov phrased it:

> The enemies of Communism portray Communists as the advocates of armed uprisings, violence, and civil war at all times and under all circumstances. This is an absurd slander against the Communists and the working class they represent. Communists and the working class, of course, prefer the most painless forms of transition from the one social system to the other.... Whether the means used are more peaceful or more violent depends not so much on the working class as on the extent and the forms of resistance used by the exploiting classes which are being overthrown and which do not wish to part voluntarily with the vast property, political power, and privileges which they possess.

Another aspect of peaceful coexistence, which must detract from whatever optimism some Western quarters may feel towards it, is the notion that peaceful coexistence actually helps the Communist-led international revolutionary process. The idea was based on Lenin's idea that peace slogans disrupt the capitalists and aid the Communists, even if Communist advocacy of peace is more "slogan" and insubstantial than the more sincere, basic ideology. It also fuels "progressive forces" in both capitalist and underdeveloped countries. There was a certain reticence in the beginning to spell out the international-revolutionary uses of the peaceful-coexistence line, either in reports to the congress or in analyses immediately after it. But by 1960, this connection was made in the Statement of the 81 Communist and Workers' Parties, adopted at the Communist conference in Moscow:

> The policy of peaceful coexistence is a policy of mobilizing the masses and launching vigorous action against the enemies of peace. Peaceful coexistence of states does not imply renunciation of class struggle ... The coexistence of states with differing social systems is a form of class struggle between Socialism and capitalism.

This link between peaceful coexistence and the worldwide class struggle in the thermonuclear age has been made on numerous occasions since 1956, and has been particularly emphasized in the 1970s. Updated editions of the *Diplomatic Dictionary* still contain the basic definition of peaceful coexistence inserted into this and several other Soviet reference books:

> Peaceful coexistence is a specific form of class struggle between Socialism and capitalism ... There is no contradiction between the policy of peaceful coexistence and the Marxist-Leninist position on the inevitable victory of Communism throughout the world.

Statements similar to the above were embodied in the new (and current) CPSU Program, adopted in 1961.

Middle East Crisis, 1956

The year 1956 was portentous for Soviet policy and relations between East and West for a number of reasons. Soviet penetration of the strategic Middle East, only indicated under Stalin, was begun in earnest under his successors and took a new and dangerous turn during the Arab-Israeli hostilities which broke out in the autumn. Whereas at the time of Stalin, the Soviets had indeed exerted pressure on the Middle East through territories *adjacent* to them (for example, Turkey, Iran, Iraq, and Pakistan), the new leaders began the modern Soviet practice of "leapfrogging" in their attempt to outflank Western defenses in the region. The Arab-Israeli War put to the test the Russians resolve to ship arms to Egypt and Syria (which they did in September 1955, through Czechoslovakia, totaling $500 million). Some observers consider the Israeli military action against Egypt to have been instigated by the Soviets, in the sense that Soviet backing and arms aid (perhaps advisers, too) encouraged Egyptian raids and incursions against Israel.

With the world's attention diverted by the anti-Communist uprisings in Hungary in October and November, Moscow turned to the Middle East and took a bold stand in Egypt's defense. Premier Bulganin warned on November 5, 1956: "We are fully determined to crush the aggressors and restore peace in the Middle East through the use of force." This statement was given in the form of Soviet letters to the British and French governments. Then, on November 10, came another shocker from Moscow: The Soviet news agency TASS announced that Communist "volunteers" might be sent into the combat area near Suez, a force estimated at 50,000 Russians plus the 250,000 Chinese proffered by Peking. The Soviets also threatened to send planes. But no volunteers were sent and no serious military preparations were undertaken in the Soviet Union, so far as anyone in the West could determine. The affair over volunteers and planes seemed to be one of a first in a series of Khrushchevian bluffs that include the Berlin crises of 1958 and 1961 and ended with the last and fatal one (for Khrushchev's political destinies), the "Cuban fiasco" of October 1962.

The result of the Arab-Israeli War of 1956, while inconclusive for either Egypt, Israel, or their futures, was, however, advantageous for the Soviet Union. It opened the way to greater Soviet influence in Egypt, then seen by the Soviets as a fulcrum for extending their influence in the area. The culmination of this was the building of the Aswan Dam with Soviet help, after the United States had been outflanked on the project. Further deals with the Egyptians followed: Russian crude oil in exchange for Egyptian cotton and rice; Czechoslovak training and equipping of Egyptian soldiers. From 1954 to 1958, trade between Egypt and Russia tripled, and Egyptian as well as Syrian trade with the East European countries also was increased. Another result of the war was that the Middle East was further divided into pro-Soviet and anti-Soviet factions, with Moscow being content to deemphasize its overt support of the subversive Communist parties in those half-dozen or so Arab countries which seemed to be the most promising places for the Russians to subvert.

In their Middle Eastern policy, the Soviets were bent upon several goals: first, geopolitical aims, or gaining a foothold in the Suez area, and in the sea lanes, in the Mediterranean, Persian Gulf, Indian Ocean, and Atlantic; second, oil, or the possibility of "shutting off the tap" which supplied Europe with almost all of its petroleum fuel; third, domination of the African continent, starting at the strategic Mediterranean littoral; fourth, classical goals of Leninism-Stalinism, or revolutionizing the imperialist rear. The successive Soviet attempts, some of which were successful, and some of which were not, to penetrate further into the Middle East between 1956 and 1976 can be traced back to this early post-Stalin period.

Sputnik I

The launch of Sputnik I, in October 1957, greatly enhanced the Soviet image in terms of dramatically illustrating the new "correlation of forces" in the "Soviet favor." In political terms, it was momentous because it showed that the Soviet Union was indeed a force to be reckoned with and not ridiculed as a backward nation. True, some people in the West went overboard. To them, the achievement of Soviet science seemed to suggest other areas of Soviet superiority, especially in the field of education. The impression that this achievement made on American political leaders was also enormous, touching off the "missile-gap" paranoia. Overlooked in all this was the fact that Sputnik had been the singular result of a special crash program, accomplished at great effort and expense by both civilians and the military.

The Russians capitalized on the achievement to advance détente with the United States, but they also brought about the long-awaited summit meeting between President Eisenhower and a Soviet head of state in the United States. Khrushchev arrived and promptly generated a degree of friendliness by conducting himself with uncustomary joviality and like a worker-become-commissar.

On one occasion, during an ebullient moment on his visit at an International Press Club luncheon, Khrushchev gave the impression that he was not particularly interested in Marxist-Leninist ideology or its projection of an idyllic future under "full communism." Nor did he seem to be particularly concerned over the other basic tenets of the ideology, least of all the notion of forcibly extending Communism throughout the world. But this was evidently a charade designed to contribute to that second apparition that "materialized" in the post-Stalin period, the "Spirit of Camp David," of 1959.

Khrushchev Policies, 1960-1964

In the last years of Khrushchev's domination over foreign and domestic policy in the Soviet Union, there was not the slightest tangible departure in the attempted realization of the basic goals of Soviet foreign policy. No revisions of basic Marxist-Leninist tactics and strategy were made. One need not confine himself to analyzing the two Khrushchev party congresses of 1959 and 1961, the 21st and 22nd, but they suffice to illustrate the point. Basic Leninism remained intact, and in some senses, was even revitalized so that it appeared more anachronistic than formerly in the age of thermonuclear-tipped ICBMs. Here are a few quotations from Khrushchev from the last party congress to be held under his leadership:

> The peoples of Asia and Africa ... seek the backing and support of the World Socialist System in the struggle against the colonists' encroachments on freedom and independence. ... Some people do not like this stand. Too bad. Such are our convictions ... Colonialism is dead and a stake will be driven into its grave. Such is the will of the people and such is the course of history.
> The contradictions that existed between the imperialist powers before the war have reappeared and new ones have

emerged. The struggle between the British and West German imperialists for supremacy in Western Europe is growing fiercer. French imperialism, in its struggle against British imperialism, is trying to find support in yesterday's enemy, the West German monopolies. This unnatural alliance—it is like a marriage of convenience—is more and more frequently operating against France herself. Major contradictions divide the U.S.A. and Britain and other imperialist states; these contradictions manifest themselves in NATO and other aggressive blocs.

It is becoming more and more obvious that the imperialist powers and their leaders fear a slackening of international tension, since in a tense situation, it is easier for them to form military blocs and keep the peoples in fear of an alleged threat from Socialist countries.

In our times, however, it has become dangerous for imperialism to seek a way out of contradictions by using war as a pressure valve.

Comrades: In the period under review [1956-61] important changes have taken place in the correlation of forces in the world arena. The World Socialist System has become the reliable shield protecting not only the peoples of the countries friendly to us, but all of mankind against the military adventures of imperialism. And the fact that the preponderance of strength rests on the side of the Socialist commonwealth of peoples is extremely fortunate for all of mankind. At the same time, the forces of peace have continued to grow all over the world.

Some pacifist-minded people in the West think in their naïveté that if the Soviet Union were to make more concessions to the Western powers, there would be no aggravation of international tension. These people fail to consider that the policy of the imperialist powers, including their foreign policy, is determined by the class interests of monopoly capital, in which aggression and war are organically embedded. When under the pressure of the masses the advocates of a more or less moderate policy win the upper hand, a relaxation of international tension occurs, the war clouds are somewhat dissipated. But when the pressure of the masses relaxes and the day is carried by those groups of the bourgeoisie who grow rich from the arms race and see in war a chance for more profit, the international atmosphere becomes aggravated.

... The greater the might of the Socialist camp and the more vigorously the fight for peace is pressed in capitalist countries themselves, the harder it is for the imperialists to carry out their aggressive aims.

Peace and peaceful coexistence are not quite the same thing. Peaceful coexistence is not simply the absence of war, not an unstable truce between wars. It is the coexistence of two opposing social systems, founded on mutual renunciation of war as a means for settling disputes between states. ... Aggressors must not be humored, therefore, but bridled.

Contacts between leaders of other countries (summitry) have come to be one of the important elements of Soviet foreign policy. As we know, V. I. Lenin, who was directly involved in guiding the foreign policy of the Soviet state, for all his busy work-schedule, used to meet with figures from the U.S., Britain, France, Finland, Afghanistan, and other countries, conducted negotiations with them, and was intending himself to participate in the Genoa Conference in 1922. The party Central Committee has made a point of steadfastly observing this tradition established by Lenin. ... Sixty-five trips to 27 non-socialist states have been made by members of the party Presidium. ... I, too, have had occasion to do quite a bit of traveling the wide world over. Nothing can be done about it; my position requires it; it is demanded in the interest of our cause. ...

Present conditions have opened up the prospect of achieving peaceful coexistence over the entire period within which the social and political problems now dividing the world must be resolved. Matters are reaching the point where even before the total victory of Socialism on earth, while capitalism holds on in part of the world, there will be a real chance of eliminating war from the life of society.

V. I. Lenin taught us to remain firm, unyielding, and uncompromising where fundamental positions of principle are at stake. Under the most trying circumstances, when the only Socialist state [the USSR] was withstanding the assaults of the whole capitalist world, when the enemy was attacking us at the front, in the rear, and on the flanks, Vladimir Ilyich used firm and resolute language with the imperialists, while at the same time pursuing a flexible line and constantly retaining the initiative.

Khrushchev's diplomacy between 1960 and 1964 was no less threatening than in the preceding years, nor did it lack the customary craftiness of its Leninist and Stalinist origins. Whether it was the two major crises over Berlin, the U-2 Incident of May 1960, the warnings to Kennedy at the summit in Vienna in 1961, breaking the moratorium on atomic explosions in 1961, or the deception over the attempted installation of offensive missiles on the island of Cuba in 1962, Khrushchev's conduct remained true to form. The "Leninist" goals, and the methods to reach them, revealed in the very opening days of Détente-I, had not changed.

Khrushchev's Policies in the Last Months

However, in the last months before he was dismissed, Khrushchev seemed to be exploring the possibility of mounting a second détente with the West, and the United States in particular. He seemed to indicate far more cooperativeness than the Russians had shown during Détente-I. Not that basic Marxist-Leninist-Stalinist motivations and goals would be forgotten. But it now seemed that the First Secretary was ready to admit that the danger to the Soviet Union represented by China, which was now bitterly waging an anti-Soviet cold war, that by no means went un-answered by the Soviet side, called for a radical overhaul of the Russians' Western policy. However, as Khrushchev clearly indicated in his memoirs (appearing in 1970), his new policy for détente was opposed by the Soviet military as well as some unnamed opponents among his civilian colleagues within the party. (One of the known opponents was Second Secretary Frol Kozlov, another was Secretary Mikhail Suslov.) In the light of those who were involved in the successful plot that finally overthrew Khrushchev in October 1964, it can be assumed that

Brezhnev, Suslov, Kosygin, and perhaps Mikoyan opposed Khrushchev's emergent policy toward the West. What was Khrushchev planning with regard to this policy?

First, he appears to have anticipated a major commercial détente with the United States to make sizable improvements in the Soviet economy by borrowing from American technological know-how. He also clearly indicated that he was prepared to reach some agreements with the United States related to military matters. Toward the latter, he signed the 1963 Test Ban Agreement, and agreed to the Hot Line in the same year (which, significantly, was criticized in print in Soviet media after his ouster). On the matter of Vietnam, also touching military affairs and American relations, Khrushchev was apparently willing to phase out Soviet support of the Vietcong, and to try to reach some peaceful end to the conflict. This could be inferred from his instructions to the Soviet delegate to the United Nations, Platon Morozov, in August 1964, to invite the combatant parties to a special meeting of the Security Council in order to present their cases. (The move was bitterly denounced, not only in Peking, but also in Hanoi.) Khrushchev also publicized parts of his new policy in the Soviet media, and it seemed to some observers that Moscow might be on the verge of abandoning its support of the "Vietnam national-liberation struggle" in favor of amity and cooperation and for avoiding the danger arising from local war. Subsequent collaboration between America and Russia might have been directed against Maoist China, or so possibly reasoned Khrushchev.

Third, Khrushchev was clearly planning a major *volte-face* with respect to Germany. Ever since 1955, when the Soviets first opened diplomatic relations with Bonn, Moscow could not manage to reach a solid *modus vivendi* and détente with West Germany because of Soviet differences with the West over the status of Berlin and with East Germany over close relations with Bonn. Khrushchev now prepared to dispatch a team of journalists to Bonn in the latter part of 1964 to try to determine the *Ostpolitik* of Chancellor Ludwig Erhard.

Finally, confirmation was forthcoming that Khrushchev was planning a major shift in domestic priorities, as far as national expenditures and resource allocation were concerned, toward the production of consumer goods. Khrushchev accordingly retired some military officers who might have opposed this, while the military counterattacked, saying that Soviet military tactics and strategy needed modernizing and that conventional arms had been neglected under Khrushchev's much-vaunted program of the "biggest bang at the least expenditure"; that is, his emphasis upon strategic rockets, his characterization of battleships as "obsolete," were all misguided since the role that could be played in the future by the Soviet Navy looked bright. If the fleet were built up and equipped to perform both its traditionally political as well as military functions, it could become a force for "showing the flag," for increasing the offensive capacities of the Soviet armed forces, and for giving substance to Soviet ideological globalism. The approaching era was fraught with danger, détente or no détente, so reasoned the military, and the correlation of forces should be "decisively" and "substantially" altered in the Soviet favor—not merely on paper, not by bluster, but in actual fact.

The anti-Khrushchev forces were finally able to oust the First Secretary by granting him a vacation to the Black Sea, where Khrushchev calmly rested without the slightest suspicion of what was awaiting him when he returned to Moscow. Then, Mikoyan joined him at Sochi, on the Black Sea, as if to make sure that Khrushchev would remain where he was. Finally, the plotters back in Moscow set their plans in motion. When Khrushchev was summoned to the capital to attend a "special meeting" of the Presidium, he was confronted with a unified demand for his ouster.

* * *

Détente-I (which was begun in 1955) did not constitute much of a precedent upon which to build Détente-II (beginning in earnest in 1969), that is, in the favorable sense of "relaxation of tension." As we have seen, the ideological factor, always aggravating conditions for tension and the course of events affecting relations between East and West, often in a negative way, seemed to lead to cold peace rather than to cooperation. However, we have also seen that as the Khrushchev period drew to a close, the First

Secretary appeared to be contemplating a change of policy, in several respects. The change appeared to be in a moderate rather than harsh direction. But this must be based largely upon conjecture: Since Khrushchev was not permitted to see his suggested new policies through to their consummation, the rest is speculation. It is possible, after all, that the deposed Soviet leader had nothing more in mind than another "zig" in the whole zigzag pattern that characterized his seven or more years in the government. On the other hand, the Khrushchev memoirs do display the discontent the leader felt toward what he considered to be more "dangerous" or "adventurist" elements existing in the Kremlin leadership. For example, he speaks contemptuously of a certain "orator," who seems to be Brezhnev, and of the military— all of whom, he strongly implies, have developed precisely those policies and those priorities since Khrushchev's ouster, which he, Khrushchev, was planning to revise.

The new regime did not hesitate to present its version of updated Marxism-Leninism, in word as well as in deed. As a consequence, the opening of Détente-II had to await the fruition of a number of measures and achievements, planned and executed by Brezhnev, Kosygin, Suslov, and Podgorny.

5

Détente-II: Its Preparation and Results

Khrushchev was deposed not only because he sought a stronger détente with the West, but because he wanted to downgrade the program of military buildup and modernization in favor of the production of consumer goods. Brezhnev immediately switched the priorities back in favor of the military. The navy was given particular attention, and Brezhnev and his spokesmen began talking about the Soviets' global manifest destiny. (Brezhnev did plan for some improvement in the standard of living, but whether his plan and accomplishment measured up to what Khrushchev seemed to have in mind is a matter of conjecture.) Brezhnev's program to modernize armaments made Khrushchev's words, of two months earlier, totally obsolete: "The country's defense is at the necessary level."

Vietnam

The Kremlin announced the decision to change Khrushchev's policy, first of all on Vietnam. Hints of stepped-up Soviet aid were made in speeches and the press. The Soviets obviously hoped to outdo the Maoists in lending support to Hanoi, thereby counting on attracting North Vietnam into a closer relationship with Moscow. The Kremlin made it increasingly clear that it would see the war through to the bitter end, regardless of the consequences this might have for relations with the United States. By 1966, the Soviet press was editorializing to the effect that the United States had been "drawn into" the war and into a dilemma, to the evident pleasure of the Kremlin. Meanwhile, Brezhnev and Kosygin had left the status of détente with the United States where Khrushchev had left it, opting instead not only for a policy of confining the United States but also "hemming in" (*potesnit'*) the United States. A Soviet press cartoon showed Lilliputians scampering over the prostrate body of Gulliver (the United States) staked to the ground by bands of "struggle" waged by North Vietnam and the Vietcong. This was not only very apt cartooning, but was reflective of Kremlin designs, which were conveniently abetted by politico-military decisions made in Washington.

By Soviet foreign-aid standards, Moscow's shipments of military hardware and other materials to Hanoi were colossal, although far under the cost of the help the United States sent to the South. Soviet aid may have reached $2 to 3 billion (as against America's over $100 billion after 1965). Soviet and Chinese threats against more decisive military assistance from the United States to the South, such as use of tactical nuclear weapons, conventional bombing of the dikes in the North, or interdicting supplies flowing into North Vietnam from Red China and the Soviet Union by land and sea, proved to be successful in confining the military action of the United States to the "tolerable" limits established by the Communists. The Chinese were known to have communicated to the United States through intermediaries (quite possibly with Soviet assistance) that hordes of Chinese troops would likely pour into the war, as they had in the Korean conflict, if the United States did any of these things. The United States, of course, never exceeded these limits, having decided, apparently, not to call what may have been a Chinese bluff in this case. Only by 1972 did the administration in Washington, under Nixon and Kissinger, take the apparently risky course of mining the harbors in Haiphong and six other ports in North Vietnam where foreign ships delivered valuable material. The United States also began its devastatingly accurate laser bombing at this time. Had both of these military innovations been continued longer, the war might have been ended to the advantage of the United States and South Vietnam, although this hypothesis admittedly lies in the realm of the "meta-historical if."

In any case, Moscow did not let the war seriously obstruct the underlying strategy and tactics for maintaining relations with the West, which had been fixed since 1952. Nor did Washington, for that matter. Even as the war raged on in the rice paddies and jungles of Vietnam, and with bomb tonnage that the Americans dropped beginning to exceed the total unleashed by the allies against enemy territory in World War II, President Johnson and Premier Kosygin agreed to hold talks in Glassboro, New Jersey, in June 1968. Kosygin's main intention at that time was to sound out Johnson *personally* on how continued Vietnam escalation by both the United States and the Soviet Union would affect their basic relations. It is possible that Moscow feared that the United States might back away from its duties in Vietnam, which would have utterly confused Soviet planning at that stage of the game. But Kosygin seemed assured that "Anglo-Saxon stubbornness," a term often used by tsarist diplomats to describe Anglo-American behavior in the world, would prevail here too, as expected.

The Russians also conducted highly secret conversations, through Gromyko, with the White House. In his Washington discussions, Gromyko reportedly kept raising the subject of China, that Maoism represented a common threat to both the United States and the Soviet Union. Gromyko's intended, as well as the resultant, effect upon Nixon may have been to abet the American fear lest China enter the Vietnam conflict. This was done to induce the United States to "unite" with the Soviet Union on the matter of containing China, or to seek some way to coordinate their policies with respect to the "barbaric" Chinese. Kissinger's and Nixon's unilateral American approach to Peking, culminating in President Nixon's visit to the People's Republic of China in February 1972, was presumably a repudiation of Gromyko's efforts to deflect the United States away from any démarche toward Communist China. America's impending "Chinese connection" surely affected Moscow's policy toward the United States, as became evident in 1969 with the opening of SALT-I and Détente-II.

During the years that had seen Kosygin meet with Johnson, and Gromyko try to win the alliance of the United States against China, the Russians had been making other, resourceful moves in the conduct of their foreign policy. They exchanged visits with the North Vietnamese and solidified relations with North Korea; they calmed the stormy relations between India and Pakistan and then began to supply them with arms. They also warned the West against spreading the Vietnam War to neighboring countries in Southeast Asia, and courted Cambodia and Burma. Moreover, they tried to achieve closer relations with the more militant anti-Israel elements in Moslem North Africa. In Europe, they attempted to "build bridges" to Gaullist France, which had all but detached itself from NATO, and to tighten discipline within the Warsaw Pact alliance while urging vigilance against the drift toward liberalization and revisionism, as had taken place in Yugoslavia. (Vietnam provided a convenient rally-round-the-flag-boys impetus to secure and abet "fraternal" unity.) Finally, top Soviet officials, including Brezhnev, began to denounce the policies of President Johnson, and the President personally.

The 23rd Party Congress, 1966

The first "de-Khrushchevization" congress, which opened in Moscow at the end of March 1966, was expected to be a dull exercise in consent at the top. While the congress may have been dull as compared, say, to the 20th Congress of 1956, it was interesting and significant nonetheless. For one thing, the speeches were far more militant in tone than would have been expected of the new "clerks" in the Kremlin. Moreover, the congress reports bristled with references to revolutionariness, which, in terms of later developments, should not have been written off in the West, as it sometimes was, as mere verbiage. Brezhnev assured the gathering that "class contradictions within the capitalist system are deepening. . . . The working class in capitalist countries faces serious difficulties and will have to wage severe battles. Many such battles lie ahead of it." He used the acerbic phrase "plundering and predatory strangler of the peoples" to describe contemporary capitalism in the United States. With reference to the international Communist movement, he referred to the foreign "armies" of Communists—suggesting Stalin's use of the term in 1952, "shock brigades"—who must step up their activities against the capitalists. Such activities would surely be met, he warned, with the "terror of reaction . . . a gigantic police machine for delivering violence." A conference of the world's Communist and workers' parties would be held soon, the new First Secretary predicted, and when it was, the new "offensive against the positions held by imperialism" and the "revolutionary process" would be stepped up.

With regard to Soviet policy toward the United States, Brezhnev stated that American imperialism was becoming increasingly dangerous. American "intervention" in the Dominican Republic illustrated this, so did "military interference into the affairs of [other] Latin American countries," not to mention America's "piratical" escalation of the war in Vietnam. Such "foul enterprises" and "exploitation of the peoples by new, even more despicable means . . . revealed American imperialism's true face. . . . Our relations with the United States have worsened as the result of American aggression in Vietnam and other aggressive activities of American imperialism. The fault for this lies with the ruling circles of the U.S.A." Then Brezhnev laid down what could be called the cold-peace or "limited-coexistence" formula, a bold hard-line departure from the last Khrushchev years, which was to govern relations with the West, and particularly those with the United States, until the reintroduction of détente in the late 1960s and early 1970s:

> As concerns the USSR, it is ready to live at peace with all countries. But it will not approve of arbitrariness on the part of the imperialists in their relations with other peoples. We have stated more than once that we are prepared to improve our relations with the U.S.A. and we now still hold to this position. But for this to happen, it will be necessary for the

U.S.A. to stop its policy of aggression. . . . Our party and state
categorically repudiate the absurd notion that the Great
Powers can improve their relations at the expense of the
interests of other countries.

In the section of his speech dealing with America, Brezhnev made
no mention of the principle of peaceful coexistence. He said only
that relations between capitalist nations, not to mention those
between Russia and the West, were being increasingly governed
by "contradictions," which were deepening.

Preceding the 23rd Party Congress, the Russians maintained a
hard stance toward the United States between 1964 and 1966.
Thus, Marshal Rodion Malinovsky stated on November 7, 1964
that

Tensions and the danger of the outbreak of a new world
war have increased.

The "capitalist imperialists" in the foreseeable future can
be counted on to launch local war, which need not necessarily
escalate into big wars and which, moreover, if they were
joined in by any of the Communist powers on the side
opposite of that of the imperialists, could be considered
"just" wars, legitimate "national-liberation wars."

Should a global conflict break out, whether or not as the
result of surprise attack by either side, the war would be a
long, drawn-out conflict, passing through many stages and
involving many types of weapons, both strategic and
conventional.

Less than parity in numbers of ICBMs in Soviet possession
would be an unsafe strategy; the Soviets must continue to
work toward superiority in this as well as in other strategic
areas so as to have an advantage over the imperialists (a link
was made with the civilian-political line on "correlation of
forces").

World War III is by no means unlikely; moreover, it could
be won by the Soviet side should the imperialists be so foolish
as to launch it; Communist victory in such a war, moreover,
would spell the end of world capitalism.

This latter statement—about capitalism's doom—revised the policy that Malenkov and Khrushchev had pursued, with certain only rare exceptions. Malenkov, and other spokesmen later during the Khrushchev years, had warned that a third world war would spell the "end of world civilization." Khrushchev, both the official Khrushchev and the unofficial Khrushchev of the memoirs, had stated that such a war would be unfortunate for the toilers, and not only for the capitalists. However, at various times in the early Khrushchev period, the First Secretary had asserted, in his more truculent moods, that capitalism would destroy itself if it ever launched the ultimate war. But now, the Soviet leaders who followed after Khrushchev suggested that World War III would be far more cataclysmic for capitalism than for Communism and that Communists could think in terms of victory. This position was stated in *Kommunist* (a journal of the Soviet Communist party) by A. A. Yepishev, Chief of the Main Political Administration of the Soviet armed forces. In it, this close ally of Brezhnev's wrote:

A third world war, should imperialism start it, would become the decisive class conflict between the two antagonistic systems. From the side of the imperialist states, this war could be the continuation of the criminal, reactionary and aggressive policies of imperialism. From the side of the Soviet Union and the countries of the Socialist Commonwealth, it would be the continuation of the revolutionary policies of freedom and independence of the Socialist state, a guarantee of the construction of Socialism and communism, and a legal as well as justified counteraction to aggression.

As we saw in Chapter 1, the party line on the true meaning of "class war" in the form of a third world war was to become merged in Soviet materials, in the 1970s, with the notion that the toilers could be spared this war through Soviet bloc efforts to "preclude," "disrupt," or "preempt" preparations for such a war. Preparations for this war, Soviet officials have claimed since 1960 and before, are underway in capitalist countries at a "feverish pace." (For the latest zag in this line, see below, pp. 169-171.)

Foreshadowing of Détente-II

The Communists continued to adhere to the old strategy of trying to split the nations of the West and thereby weaken their defenses. As we have seen, they saw a chance to do this when de Gaulle came to power once again in France. The Russians had decided to build diplomatic bridges to the French because France had become the weakest link in NATO. Perhaps they could be easily lured away thus disrupting NATO and Western defenses. Once France was won over, perhaps the Germans could more easily be lured away from the West. Eventually, the United States might be completely excluded from Europe (although the Soviets would think twice before excluding the United States from the four-power "Watch on the Reich").

The Russians accordingly decided to invite de Gaulle to Moscow in 1966. The talks that were held considered matters relating to trade and military affairs, but the Russians also promoted pan-Europism, which was a favorite cause of de Gaulle's. De Gaulle finally did withdraw from NATO's integrated military organization, in July 1966. But the Russians did not stop there. They realized that, in 1969, the 20-year term of the treaty setting up NATO was to expire. The Russians asked themselves what better way there was to encourage other nations to turn from NATO than to create the atmosphere of peace in the world, and this through détente. Thus the Russians began their campaign by harnessing the apparent momentum generated by the de Gaulle visit and the announced plan for a subsequent Brezhnev visit to Paris, with the Soviet-inspired Bucharest Declaration of July 1966, which contained several hints of an emergent second détente, with Europe being the prime motivation or "target." A first requirement for an all-European agreement (and it was by no means sure at this time that the Soviets would accept participation in it by the United States and Canada) was that the Federal Republic of Germany specifically recognize the permanence of the post-World War II eastern borders, the partition of Germany agreed to at Potsdam in 1945, and West Germany's continuing nonnuclear status. The Berlin problem, for the moment, was left unclear. The second important part of the declaration concerned the possible "dissolution" of both military organizations, of the Warsaw Pact alliance and of NATO. The Western negotiators immediately recognized the second requirement as the same that had been offered as a condition of détente in 1955. It was offered with little sincerity then, at a time when Moscow sought to improve the military strength of the Soviet bloc, and they felt that it had no more sincerity in 1966, when a huge new militarization program was underway in the Soviet Union and the Warsaw Pact alliance.

The Russians failed in their effort to create an atmosphere of détente in the mid-1960s, but they soon saw what could become another opportunity to disrupt NATO when Willy Brandt and the German Social Democrats gained political strength. The Brezhnev regime had taken a hard line on West Germany after October 1964, despite the fact that the government in Bonn was headed by a moderate Christian Democrat not normally considered as rigid as, say, Konrad Adenauer, on matters of *Ostpolitik*. Still, the new Brezhnev regime set aside those efforts by Khrushchev to open a window to Bonn, as had been originally but only partially undertaken way back in 1955. It appeared to be Brezhnev's short-term strategy to encircle Germany, as it were, by relying on his new relationship with the West. But in late 1966, the German Social Democrats, led by Willy Brandt, finally won enough votes in the Bundestag elections of November 1966 for the German Social Democrats to enter the new coalition government headed by George Kiesinger. Was it now not time to try for some long-lasting agreements with the Germans?

In late 1966, however, relations with Germany were threatened because at this stage Germany allegedly held a deeply rooted militarism, and it continued to make claims to the annexed German territories ("revanchism"). Further, even if friendship with Germany could be established, it might cause tension between the Soviets and the East Germans, who stood to gain little if anything from West German entente with the Soviet Union. Poland also objected on the basis of blunt, domestic political considerations: the Germans had openly encouraged the relationship between Poland and Russia and with it, one-party rule in Poland. The two formidable bloc opponents, the largest East European country of Poland and the economically most flourishing one, the German Democratic Republic, brought what appeared to be an emerging Soviet effort toward Bonn to a halt, at least by 1968.

Some disagreement also appeared to arise inside the Kremlin over the issue. Unity of the Soviet bloc was to get the first priority, at least for the present. Soviet concern over the possible "centrifugality" (especially in the case of Rumania) that might result from a "German connection" weighed heavier at this time than a rapprochement with Germany on the French model.

In the meantime, Moscow resumed its advocacy of pan-European security. At the Karlovy Vary conference of the European Communist parties in April 1967, the substitution of pan-European security arrangements for both NATO and the Warsaw Pact Alliance was written into the communiqué following the conference. However, instead of maintaining a system of mutual guarantees among the nations of both the East and West, Moscow now spoke of *joint big power guarantees,* on the part of the four victorious powers in World War II, against West German aggression. The notion of a four-power Watch on the Reich was scarcely new in Soviet policy, but it looked like a reversal of what had seemed to have been the policy months before, and of what was surely being considered as Soviet policy towards Germany in the last months of the Khrushchev regime.

At this point, the loyal members of the bloc began to exert pressure on Czechoslovakia to begin to conform to Moscow's rule once again. They tried to induce Czechoslovakia to do so by claiming that they risked German revanchism and invasion if it turned away from Russia. Because the Czechs did not comply, five members of the bloc invaded the country, to preclude the danger Germany supposedly posed to Czechoslovakia. In addition, this became one of the factors that motivated the Russians to publish the "Brezhnev Doctrine" in August 1968.

But shortly after the alarm over Czechoslovakia had dissipated in both the East and the West, some other developments indicated that the Russians once again were considering détente with West Germany. One of these was clearly Willy Brandt's accession to power in December 1969; another was the West German signing of the 1968 Nuclear Nonproliferation Treaty. The latter greatly reduced the danger of future West German acquisition of the ultimate weapons, seen as a sure stimulus to its alleged "aggressiveness." In any case, it was clear to officials of both East and West that the Federal Republic of Germany was neither willing nor able, politically, to pursue a truly aggressive anti-Soviet and anti-Communist policy toward the East.

Rumania was the first Soviet bloc nation to establish diplomatic relations with the Federal Republic of Germany, in 1969—a move that was at first roundly attacked in the media of Poland and East Germany, and even in the Soviet Union. But the Soviets had conducted talks at the end of 1968 on possible joint renunciation of the use of force in the relations between the two countries, which could lead to eventual détente.

There were other developments that encouraged the Russians to adopt a policy of détente. The NATO forces indicated that pan-European military security and détente could be achieved together by means of mutual force reductions, trade, and a new pan-European atmosphere of cooperation (including the United States and Canada). In addition the Security Council passed Resolution 255 providing for Permanent Members of the Security Council which possessed nuclear weapons to take jointly the necessary measures to stop any other state from undertaking nuclear aggression—by removing such a threat or thwarting any aggression already begun. Then President Johnson offered to discuss strategic arms limitation, or SALT, and finally President Nixon began to disengage the United States from Vietnam in August 1969. As a result of these developments, Foreign Minister Gromyko stated, during a speech in July 1969, that the United States and the Soviet Union could work toward a "common language" when it came to the maintenance of world peace—perhaps the first signal introducing Détente-II.

These and other events (most likely including the Sino-Soviet border clashes of early 1969) led the Russians to begin talks with the Germans in Moscow on December 8, 1969. As a follow-up, on December 16 the United States, Britain, and France renewed their long-standing offer to discuss the Berlin problem realistically with the Soviets. By this time the Russians comported themselves, in official statements, as if they felt more secure about security in Central Europe in the wake of their occupation of Czechoslovakia and the accession to power in Bonn of Willy Brandt. Brandt's *Ostpolitik* suggested to the Soviets a new opportunity for them to

bolster relations with Germany. Moscow now ignored the objec-
tions of Poland and East Germany to their approaching West
Germany (a process which was expedited by the retirement of
Walter Ulbricht in East Germany and Wladislaw Gomulka in
Poland). The unprecedented "shirt-sleeves" summit in the Crimea
on the Black Sea between the German Chancellor and the Soviet
General Secretary took place in September 1971. Professor Ulam,
of Harvard, speculated in *Expansion and Coexistence: Soviet
Foreign Policy 1917-73* (1974) that the rapprochement between
Germany and the Soviet Union was the product of a policy
followed by Brezhnev and Kosygin of "patient diplomacy," by
which West Germany would grow accustomed to being good
neighbors with the Soviet Union. The result of this, Moscow
reasoned, would be less German dependence upon the United
States in either the military or economic sphere. Moreover, the
Soviets would benefit from a refurbished image of respectability
which would aid Communist vote-gathering efforts in France and
Italy. "With Russia no longer feared," observed Ulam, "other left-
wing forces [in France and Italy] would not balk at the idea of
Communists as potential partners in government."

Soviet Preoccupation with America

Moscow's new, emerging relationship with the United States in
1969 and 1970 was also complex, as to both motivation and
strategy. Lenin had always expressed the thought that America,
among all capitalist nations, was of primary concern to Russian
policy-makers. The founder of the Soviet state was not only aware
of America's growing power during and after World War I, but
apparently also sensed, what his successors surely did, that
America's quasi-classless society, strong "bourgeois-democratic"
traditions, well-developed economy, hatred of tyranny "in any
form," and antisocialist bent, which persistently thwarted Communist chances in the United States of even forming a labor party,
all made America problematic and "interesting" to the Soviets. In
the post-World War II epoch, America's place in the Soviet
scheme of things assumed transcending importance. This became
true even more after the United States had developed and

perfected nuclear weapons and rocket-delivery systems. But the Russians also realized that the United States had become the nucleus around which the burden of anti-Communism had crystallized; America had become the "No. 1 adversary" of the Soviet Union in the cold war.

Soviet strategy was developed to isolate the United States, which is geographically a kind of island, from the rest of the Western world. Then the Soviets would slowly erode the Western institutions for defense, either as they exist in individual Western countries or in NATO, and to do this either by pillorying the United States as the chief threat to world peace (the explicitly stated Soviet ploy from 1956 until Khrushchev's overthrow which was continued and even stepped up until the present), or by pointing out that a profound "shift in the correlation of forces," East and West, has taken place in which even the United States is allegedly overpowered. The shift could be impressed on the consciousness of the world, to use the Leninist expression, not only by breaking the moratorium on nuclear testing by conspicuously detonating a huge device, as Khrushchev did in 1961, by conducting gigantic global military exercises, as Brezhnev did, or by advertising military buildup, as the Russians wanted to do through SALT and its accompanying communiqués, but also by *showing the whole world a weapon-by-weapon, missile-by-missile count of the growing Soviet strength.* Once the world became accustomed to Soviet "nuclear parity with the U.S.," a good many of the noncommitted, as well as the committed countries in the West, might reconsider cold-war militancy to be too dangerous a game and one sponsored mainly by Americans. Meanwhile, Moscow would "welcome" burial of the cold war.

The 24th Party Congress, 1971

This 24th Party Congress was convened in March 1971 in an era that was markedly different from that of the 23rd. Recapitulation of these altered circumstances, and the policies and events in the East and West that accompanied them, illustrate this. Certainly, the relations between Russia and Germany had changed. The Treaty of Moscow, August 12, 1970, had been signed, which one historian of East-West diplomacy described not only as a *de jure* coming to terms between West Germany and its old enemy, the Soviet Union, but as a *"de facto* European peace settlement." Although not ratified until two years later by the Bundestag in Bonn, the treaty led to agreements over Berlin, which seemed to eliminate what Foreign Minister Gromyko described to the Supreme Soviet in July 1969 as an approaching era in which dangerous confrontation between the East and West could be terminated. The Berlin settlement was made in the Quadripartite Agreement of September 1973, which provided, among other things, for unimpeded traffic between the eastern and western sectors of the city and the Federal Republic of Germany, and for some relaxation of Soviet opposition to concrete political ties between West Berlin and Bonn (for example, the Federal Republic of Germany established consular services in the western sectors and began to represent the interests of the western sectors at international conferences). (A treaty between East and West Germany was signed in 1972, and the treaty between the Federal Republic of Germany and Czechoslovakia renouncing the 1938 Munich agreement was agreed upon in 1973.)

The attitude of the members of NATO toward the Soviet-backed plan for a pan-European security conference had also changed. Such a conference, the West reasoned, might open the way toward freer movement of people across the borders between the East and West, an exchange of ideas on a freer basis (in the East) than previously had existed, and various nonpolitical forms of governmental and economic cooperation, in the realms of commerce, ecology, scientific knowledge, and so on.

Relations with the Chinese had changed as well. There had been bloody border clashes with the Chinese in the spring and summer of 1969. For some observers, these incidents impelled the Soviet Union to endeavor to secure its "Western rear." Russia, largely a landlocked power, always had been concerned that she might get caught in an East-West squeeze whereby an enemy in the Far East would drive westward while an enemy at the western gate drove eastward, as had happened during the Second World War when Germany attacked Russia from the West and Japan menaced it from the East. But that was probably only part of the story, and not the most important part at that.

Of overriding importance on the eve of the 24th Party Congress was the possibility of opening a whole new phase of relaxation of tension, the policy the Russians had followed since the days of Stalin and that had become stalled for a time after the fall of Khrushchev and the commitment of the Soviet Union and the United States in the Vietnam War. But it appeared to be once again timely and applicable to Soviet foreign policy. Accordingly, in the main reports to the 24th Party Congress, the Soviet "Program of Peace" became one of the dominant themes, so far as the foreign arena was concerned. Also related to the updating of post-Stalinist détente, and the emergent special détente with the United States, was the important third conference of the world Communists, held in Moscow during June 1969. And before analyzing the Program of Peace and other themes at the 1971 Congress, the theses established by this conference must be kept in mind since they constitute an important inspiration to the congress, where several important references were made to them.

The setting for World Conference III was suggestive of what was to follow: St. George's Hall of the Great Kremlin Palace with its many associations with tsarist history and Russian military exploits. Representing 75 parties and meeting for over ten days (June 5 to 17, 1969), the conference updated the Comintern-Cominform line from the last conference held in 1960 and asserted traditional Russian interests. However, the Italian, British, Rumanian, Australian, and several other delegations hinted, not too subtly, that each party's independence would not be sacrificed to the Soviet understanding of "internationalism." Moreover, Ceausescu made a strong appeal at the conference for the principle of inviolability of national sovereignty—the Rumanian leader's obvious repudiation of the Brezhnev Doctrine as applied to the sovereignty of Czechoslovakia in August 1968. The Italians, not unexpectedly, displayed a nostalgia for Togliatti's theory of "polycentrism," as they frankly condemned any type of "hegemonism" within the international Communist movement. For this reason, World Communist Conference III was something less than a success from the Soviet point of view, especially since not all the Communist parties could bring themselves to sign the final declaration. Despite the lack of unanimity, or because of it, the Soviet delegation, and the delegations especially loyal to it, for example, from the Northern Tier, made an extremely strong assertion of traditional Cominternism.

At this conference, Brezhnev also excoriated Mao for his "despicable heedlessness and cynicism [who] spoke in this same hall [in 1957] about the possible destruction of half of mankind in the case of atomic war." Brezhnev went on: "The fact is that Mao Tse-tungism calls for a struggle not against war, but for war, which is regarded as having positive historical significance."

But, again, the conference was less than successful, for not all the delegates agreed with the condemnation of China. The Rumanian party leader, Ceaucescu, even reported that his delegation had considered staging a walkout in protest against the attack.

It was at this conference, too, that Brezhnev reopened the possibility of forming a special relationship with the United States when he said:

We have here no exceptions [in the application of the policy of peaceful coexistence] to any of the capitalist states, including the U.S.A. Peaceful coexistence is for us not a temporary tactical device but an important principle of a consistently peaceloving Socialist foreign policy.

This singling out of the United States by Brezhnev was echoed a month later, in July 1969, in the speech of Gromyko to the Supreme Soviet. The Soviet Foreign Minister said that his government "had always attached great importance to relations with the United States," despite obvious "profound class differences" between the two nations and societies. The foreign minister referred to the possible "common language" which the two nations henceforth could speak with one another as they avoided confrontations. Most significantly, Gromyko predicted that summits with the United States might take place in the near future. The fact that Moscow was in earnest in the desire to develop some new détente with the United States was indicated in an article placed by high party authorities within the pages of the journal of the Soviet-USA Institute, *S.Sh.A. (U.S.A.)* for January 1970. One of the most significant sections of the piece, written by no less a personage than the daughter of the Soviet Premier Kosygin, Lydia Gvishiani, went as follows:

Lenin announced the possibility of reaching agreement with the capitalist countries, the first and foremost among them being the United States. Decisions made by Vladimir Ilyich Lenin in the sphere of foreign policy might appear, to dogmatists, to be too bold. As G. V. Chicherin wrote [in 1919], "For all of us, a sudden change from the previous opinions expressed by an underground revolutionary party to one of political realism of a government in power was extremely difficult."

At the 24th Party Congress in Moscow, held in 1971, one might have expected a major *volte-face* toward America on the part of the Russians. SALT had been underway since late 1969; the Non-Proliferation Treaty had been ratified by March 1970 by the three major signers, the United States, Britain, and the Soviet Union. Unfortunately, the war in Vietnam had not been fully terminated, while the Middle East continued to be one of the world's major crisis points. As to the latter, Moscow reverted to the policy begun in 1956. This took the form, in January 1970, of sending to Egypt over a hundred MIGs, 300 SAMs (surface-to-air missiles), and other military supplies. For these reasons, Brezhnev was extremely restrained at the 1971 party congress on the matter of détente with the United States. In the opening segment of his report on international affairs, made on March 30, the priorities were assigned to topics worded as follows:

1. For the Further Development of Friendship and Cooperation by the Socialist Countries
2. Imperialism—Enemy of the Peoples and Social Progress. The Peoples Against Imperialism
3. The Struggle by the Soviet Union for Peace and the Peoples' Security. Opposition to the Imperialist Policy of Aggression.

In other words, there was no separately headed section in which Brezhnev discussed détente. However in the report on the international situation, the General Secretary said:

Now about relations of the Soviet Union with the United

States of America. Improvement in Soviet-American relations would serve the interests of the Soviet and American
peoples as well as the interests of lasting peace. However, we
cannot ignore the aggressive activities of the U.S.A. in
various parts of the world. In recent times, the American
administration has hardened its position on a number of
international issues, among which are those which impinge
on the interests of the USSR. Complicating the conduct of
affairs with the United States are the frequent zigzags in
American foreign policy. These, obviously, are connected
with the various internal political maneuverings of a competitive [electoral] nature.

We base ourselves on the fact that improvement in
relations between the USSR and the U.S.A. is possible. Our
fundamental line on such relations with capitalist countries,
including the U.S.A., consists in the fact of fully and
consistently abiding in practice by the principles of peaceful
coexistence in developing mutually profitable relations,
while, with those countries who also strive for it, to cooperate
for the purpose of strengthening peace, lending the greatest
possible permanency to such relations. But we must take into
account the question of whether we are dealing with sincere
[capitalist] attempts to reach agreement on questions at the
negotiating table or merely with attempts to follow the
[capitalist-imperialist] policy of "position of strength."

Each time the imperialists have sought to conceal their
aggressive undertakings, they have resorted to resurrecting
the myth about the "Soviet threat." They look for the signs of
such a threat in the Indian Ocean, or on the plateaus of the
Cordilleras. Or, for that matter, in European ravines, where if
you look through binoculars made by NATO, all you will see
are Soviet divisions waiting to pounce on the West.

But ascribing such intentions to the Soviet Union, for
whom they are entirely foreign, does not deceive the peoples.
With total responsibility we hereby state: We have no
territorial ambitions anywhere; we threaten no one; we are
not preparing to attack anywhere; and we stand for the free
and independent development of all peoples. But, let no one
speak to us the language of ultimatums and force.

And at the very end of his address, Brezhnev reintroduced the "Cominternist" line. Here, Brezhnev spoke of the Soviet intention "as before to conduct a decisive struggle against imperialism, to deliver a firm rebuff to plots and diversions of aggressors. Also as before, we will in every respect support the struggle of the peoples for democracy, national liberation, and Socialism."

In the same vein, Brezhnev strongly supported a variety of Communist efforts abroad. Here the *"three basic revolutionary forces of our day"* were described: *Socialism, the international workers' movement,* and *national-liberation struggle.* And the report on the congress by *Pravda* emphasized the "stepped-up" class struggle in the United States, the spread of unrest throughout Western Europe brought on by inflation and strikes, and the supreme internationalist task of achieving solidarity within the world Communist movement.

The message was that while détente with West Europe had favorably affected the relations of the Soviet Union with capitalist countries, Soviet support and defense of social, and "proletarian," workers' interests in those countries remained unaffected by détente. At the 25th Party Congress in 1976, as we have already mentioned, Brezhnev updated this notion in stating that détente, to the Soviets, could never mean acceptance of the status quo with regard to the "class structure" inside capitalist countries, with whom the Soviet Union could nevertheless have diplomatic and other kinds of relations. In other words, the "double-track" or *diopezza* nature of Soviet foreign policy, of peaceful coexistence *and* of détente, would continue.

At the 24th Party Congress, Brezhnev also unwrapped the Program of Peace, which has been part of Soviet foreign policy ever since. (Spokesmen have said that the 25th Congress in February and March 1976 marked the continuation and "deepening" of this 1971 Brezhnev Program of Peace.) The most important parts of the Program were described by Brezhnev as follows in the General Secretary's report to the 24th Congress:

The Soviet Union has countered the aggressive policy of imperialism with its policy of active defence of peace and strengthening of international security. The main lines of this policy are well known. Our party, our Soviet state, in cooperation with the fraternal Socialist countries and other peace-loving states, and with the wholehearted support of many millions of people throughout the world, have now for many years been waging a struggle on these lines, taking a stand for the cause of peace and friendship among nations. The CPSU regards the following as the basic concrete tasks of this struggle in the present situation:

1. To eliminate the hotbeds of war in Southeast Asia and in the Middle East, and to promote a political settlement in these areas on the basis of respect for the legitimate rights of states and peoples subjected to aggression.

To give an immediate and firm rebuff to any acts of aggression and international arbitrariness. For this, full use must also be made of the possibilities of the United Nations.

To repudiate the threat or use of force in settling outstanding issues must become a law of international life. For its part, the Soviet Union invites the countries which accept this approach to conclude appropriate bilateral or regional treaties.

2. To proceed from the final recognition of the territorial changes that took place in Europe as a result of the Second World War. To bring about a radical turn towards détente and peace on this continent. To ensure the convocation and success of an all-European conference.

To do everything to ensure collective security in Europe. We reaffirm the readiness expressed jointly by the participants in the defensive Warsaw Treaty to have a simultaneous annulment of this treaty and of the North Atlantic alliance, or—as a first step—dismantling of their military organizations.

3. To conclude treaties putting a ban on nuclear, chemical, and bacteriological weapons.

To work for an end to the testing of nuclear weapons, including underground tests, by everyone everywhere.

To promote the establishment of nuclear-free zones in various parts of the world.

We stand for the nuclear disarmament of all states in possession of nuclear weapons, and for the convocation for these purposes of a conference of the five nuclear powers—the USSR, the U.S.A., the F.R.G., France, and Britain.

4. To invigorate the struggle to halt the race in all types of weapons. We favor the convocation of a world conference to consider disarmament questions to their full extent.

We stand for the dismantling of foreign military bases. We stand for a reduction of armed forces and armaments in areas where the military confrontation is especially dangerous, above all in Central Europe.

We consider it advisable to work out measures reducing the probability of an accidental outbreak or deliberate fabrication of armed incidents and their development into international crises, into war.

The Soviet Union is prepared to negotiate agreements on reducing military expenditures, above all by the major powers.

5. The U.N. decisions on the abolition of the remaining colonial regimes must be fully carried out. Manifestations of racism and apartheid must be universally condemned and boycotted.

6. The Soviet Union is prepared to expand relations of mutually advantageous cooperation in every sphere with states which for their part seek to do so. Our country is prepared to participate together with the other states concerned in settling problems like the conservation of the environment, development of power and other natural resources, development of transport and communications, prevention and eradication of the most dangerous and widespread diseases, and the exploration and development of outer space and the world ocean.

Such are the main features of the Program for the struggle for peace and international cooperation, for the freedom and independence of nations, which our Party has put forward.

And we declare that, while consistently pursuing its policy of peace and friendship among nations, the Soviet Union will continue to conduct a resolute struggle against imperialism, and firmly to rebuff the evil designs and subversions of aggressors. As in the past, we shall give undeviating support to the peoples' struggle for democracy, national liberation, and Socialism.

ORDER OF PRIORITIES IN SOVIET POLICY

Aims	*Means*
1. *Domestic security and defense of the USSR*	Slow, noticeable rise in standard of living (persuasion)
	Ideological indoctrination (persuasion)
	Rooting out of dissidence and heterodoxy (coercion)
	Relatively smooth leadership succession
	Strengthening of party dictatorship
	Criminal Code and "GULag" (coercion)
	Foreign activities of KGB and GRU
	Quasi-militarization of Soviet life
	Buildup, modernization of defenses
2. *Economic and military strength of Soviet Bloc*	Warsaw Pact Treaty Organization
	Council for Mutual Economic Assistance
	Political Consultative Committee
	Pan-bloc military coordination and exercises
	"Brezhnev Doctrine"
	Ideological conformity/CPSU "Cominternism"
	Weakening of NATO
	East-West trade

Aims	*Means*
3. *Success of "World Revolutionary Process"*	Peaceful coexistence and détente
	Monetary and military aid to CPs or allied organizations in capitalist, colonial, and ex-colonial countries
	International organizations, including U.N.
	Isolating U.S. as citadel of "reaction" and weakening of NATO
	Isolating Maoist China as ally of "reaction"
	Cominternism
4. *Controls over proliferation of nuclear weapons*	Treaties (e.g., 1968 Non-proliferation Treaty)
	U.S.-Soviet "dyarchical" arrangements
	Intelligence inputs (including those supplied by U.S. intelligence)
	Coordination of policy over sales of reactors to non-nuclear powers
	Cosmos reconnaissance satellites
5. *Soviet choice of time and place for military conflict or crisis points*	U.S.-Soviet "Hot Line"
	Infra-structures for rapid negotiation (e.g., East-West bilateral agreements)
	Foreign "ears to the ground"
	First-strike advantage

Aims	*Means*

6. *Long-standing Russian*   Arab-Soviet agreements,
   "geopolitical" targets   especially those of Soviet
                                   strategic importance (oil,
                                   naval bases)
                                Softening up of NATO,
                                   especially "periphery"
                                   (Mediterranean, Western
                                   Pacific, Indian Ocean, etc.)
                                Extension of "Zone of Peace"
                                Enhancing Far Eastern
                                   influence ("Eastern
                                   Eurasian extension" of
                                   Heartland)
                                Naval presence at key
                                   waterways (Suez, Strait of
                                   Malacca, Korean Strait,
                                   Dardanelles-Gibraltar, etc.)

U.S.-Soviet Détente, 1971-1976

The Russians continued their efforts to establish détente with
the United States when, on October 12, 1971, they invited
President Nixon to visit the Soviet Union. Nixon, accordingly,
arrived in Moscow in May 1972 for talks that lasted from May 22
to 29. The visit was given extremely heavy coverage in Soviet
media, with large page-one headlines and equally large photo-
graphs showing the President signing the various documents while
the whole Politburo stood by, as though to witness or unanimously approve the event. No other Western leader had ever
been accorded this degree of press attention. Several agreements
were signed, relating to the first stage in the SALT talks (known as
SALT-I); environmental cooperation; the planned mutual dock-
ing of American and Soviet spacecraft (the Apollo-Soyuz mission); measures for preventing dangerous "brushes" in the air or

on the seas between American and Soviet planes and ships; and joint efforts to step up trade between the two countries, which actually entailed greatly increased exports by the United States to the Soviet Union (since Soviet goods are in relatively little demand in the United States).

The trade agreement was especially important to the Soviet Union because the Soviets clearly needed advanced American technology to modernize their economy. Also, the Russians brought in a poor harvest in 1971, and the projections for the harvest in 1972 looked no better. The result was the purchase of nearly 19 million tons of grain from America. For continuing and underwriting such purchases in the future, détente would be a valuable guarantee. Moscow also sought the M.F.N. (Most Favored Nation) status enjoyed by a few other friendly Communist nations, one of the first of which, Yugoslavia, had profited from these arrangements with the United States for many years.

On the American side, Nixon hoped for Soviet cooperation in ending the war in Vietnam. The Russians agreed to intercede, and Hanoi elected to go seriously to the negotiating table. The results are well known: delays over the size and shape of the negotiating table; cheating on the agreements which were finally reached, as regular troops from North Vietnam swarmed over South Vietnamese cities. What appears in retrospect to have been a jointly devised plot by Hanoi and Moscow to win South Vietnam decisively by force in 1972 and 1973 was, in an important sense, buoyed up and made possible when détente and the summit talks were begun in timely sequence with the years of the "successful conclusion" of the Paris Vietnam peace conference and the accords finally signed in January 1973. The United States, on its part, also sought to exploit the bilateral détente, when Washington decided to mine Hanoi's ports in May 1972 and to resume heavy bombing of Hanoi in December, without expecting, under the cover of détente, a military reaction from the Soviet Union. (As mentioned above, the effective use of American mining techniques and laser-beam bombing raids against the Communists constituted new, serious threats to a Communist victory in Vietnam.) Thus, Hanoi, Moscow, and Peking, all three of whom cooperated in Vietnam at that time, were disposed to act carefully lest détente, the emerging Paris peace accords, and the "game" in

Vietnam all be lost. The Communist powers duly exercised restraint while Washington got its troops out of Vietnam.

One of the most significant parts of the Moscow summit agreements was the Joint Declaration of Basic Principles of Relations Between the USSR and the U.S.A. This constituted a preamble introducing all the various accords that followed in the documents. It was intended, apparently, to anchor relations with the United States to a foundation of fundamentals governing the world's superpower dyarchy. What the Basic Principles asserted, in effect, was that the two mightiest powers on the globe would collaborate in "preventing the development of situations capable of causing a dangerous exacerbation of their relations," a kind of duopolistic "Security Council." And other powers sought to disturb the peace being kept and supervised by two superpowers, both might intervene together to eliminate the danger. The principles also obliged the United States and the Soviet Union to avoid situations in which they might become embroiled with each other. Nor would they play the dangerous game in world politics with arms or any other support to one or another side in preparing or launching a local war. In the light of the events that followed soon after the signing of the Joint Declaration of Basic Principles—for example, in the Middle East, where an arms race continued to develop apace as the Soviets initiated and the United States perforce matched the successive arms buildups in the area—the preamble of the 1972 Moscow summit accords stood like a beacon shining in an abandoned cove.

Brezhnev's return visit to the United States took place between June 18 and 25, 1973. Once again, Soviet newspapers carefully restricted their reprinting of the "tour" of the United States (far more limited in scope, for example, than that of Khrushchev in 1959). Brezhnev's remarks, in his address to the 24th Party Congress in 1971, that the imperialists customarily mask their aggressive plans by invoking the Soviet threat, seemed to take on an ironic double twist when it is realized that during the friendly talks between President Nixon and General Secretary Brezhnev, Soviet planning went ahead on preparations for Soviet assistance and advice in the joint Egyptian-Syrian Yom Kippur attack on Israel that lay just three months ahead. A similarly dialectical approach was taken to deal with the emerging oil crises, which finally culminated that December, as the Arab countries, strongly supported in word and deed by the Soviet bloc, quadrupled the price of oil.

But as they were concluded, the Nixon-Brezhnev talks produced epoch-making agreements (although they had been jointly prepared long in advance by officials of the Soviet Ministry of Foreign Affairs). Among these were accords on SALT; lessening tensions; seeking additional collective security agreements (culminating in the Helsinki Accords of August 1975); commerce; environment; research in the World Ocean; peaceful use of atomic energy; agriculture; and augmented airline service.

There was also the special U.S.-Soviet Agreement on Prevention of Nuclear War, signed June 22, 1973. In some respects, this agreement completed the earlier Moscow 1972 Joint Declaration, particularly the passages of the former agreement dealing with the responsibility of the United States and the Soviet Union for avoiding military confrontations. In the 1973 Washington agreement, apparently as the result of Soviet initiative, the two sides agreed to "proceed from the premise that each party will refrain from the threat or use of force against the other party, against the allies of the other party, and against other countries, in circumstances which may endanger international peace and security." The following important additional provision appeared in the new agreement:

> If at any time relations between the parties or between either party and other countries appear to involve the risk of a nuclear war between the U.S.A. and the USSR or between either party and other countries, the United States and the Soviet Union, acting in accordance with the provisions of this agreement, will immediately enter into urgent consultations with each other and make every effort to avert this risk.

The wording of Article IV of the Agreement on Prevention of Nuclear War suggests that if the Soviet Union were approaching the brink of a hot war with, say, Red China, Moscow would be obliged to enter into consultations with Washington to preclude the opening of hostilities (which would likely involve nuclear weapons, since both China and Russia are members of the nuclear league). This might cast the United States into the role of a mediator, analogous to the role it played during the Russo-Japanese War of 1904 and 1905. This war had been terminated largely through the efforts of the United States acting as go-between for the two warring powers; the treaty ending the war was signed in Portsmouth, New Hampshire. A second possibility might be a situation in which the United States expected to be consulted by Moscow but was not, as the Soviets launched a surprise invasion of, say, Red China. By the time any "consultation" could be undertaken, the Soviets would most likely enjoy an advantageous military position in the opening phase of the hostilities. The American expectation that it would be consulted by the other side might thus "neutralize" the United States on the eve of a Soviet decision to attack some other country and paralyze American intervention after the attack.

A third situation might find the Soviets employing an ultimatum against another power—a form of nuclear extortion—while at the same time offering to "consult" with the United States. This situation has several precedents in the history of Soviet diplomacy. In the Finno-Soviet negotiations at the end of 1939, for example, Finland refused to yield to Soviet territorial demands and an implied ultimatum. Suddenly, the Soviet Union launched a sneak attack against the Baltic country. With part of the victimized country occupied, Moscow then proposed that negotiations and consultations be reopened. The Finns refused, the war proceeded and reached what appeared to be a near stalemate, until the huge numbers of Russian troops and quantities of equipment overcame the Finns. In this case, the gun had been loaded and fired and territory invaded. Only after this was the offer made to negotiate, but under the new and extreme conditions and pressures of war. On a smaller scale, a similar occurrence took place in Budapest during the anti-Communist revolution of the autumn of 1956. At a crucial point in what pro-Communists call the 1956 "counterrevolution" in Hungary, the Soviets invited representatives of the rebels and of the newly-installed Nagy regime to engage in meaningful talks with the Soviets, who were holding off their tanks on the outskirts of the capital. As the talks went on, the Soviets secretly regrouped and prepared to strike. As they proceeded to crush the revolt, the Russians took some of the rebel negotiators prisoner, not unlike the way they had arrested and imprisoned members of the freely-elected Constituent Assembly of January 1918, which had been permitted to meet for only a single day, or captured the members of the Dubcek government in Czechoslovakia in August 1968. Talks, consultations, "negotiations" had thus been a stalling tactic to gain a breathing space for executing a decisive attack.

But there is a less dire and pessimistic interpretation of Article IV that would run along the following lines. All of the agreements that the Russians and Americans had made, from the one against proliferation of nuclear weapons to the agreement on prevention of nuclear war between any powers throughout the world, may be viewed from this perspective: The world's dyarchs are mutually committed to preventing themselves, or others, from destroying the world. This is tied in with the declared Soviet intention not to let ideological differences between East and West, anti-capitalist struggle, or national-liberation struggle become causal elements in an apocalyptic armed conflict fought with nuclear weapons. Nevertheless, under Malenkov, Khrushchev, and Brezhnev and Kosygin, Moscow has maintained that the status quo worldwide—namely, retention of colonialism or the capitalist system anywhere in the world—should not be confused with arrangements between states under peaceful coexistence and détente. However, Moscow has at times also indicated that a third world war would bring so much devastation to the very fruits of proletarian labor, not to mention world civilization, that not even a Socialist victory would be worth that much sacrifice. Nevertheless, the overall Soviet position on this question stated during the 1970s does not leave much ground for optimism. The gist of the present Soviet position can be itemized as follows:

If the victory in a third world war were a Maoist victory, or an imperialist one, it distinctly would not be worth it.

But if the victory were a Soviet one, a third world war would have been a just, class war in which capitalism at last would be destroyed.

Since the USSR and its allies would never initiate such a war, a third world war would of necessity be a deliberately destructive war or a plundering war since only the imperialists would initiate it; once launched, however, it would be rapidly converted into a liberation war *assuming that it were not prevented ("precluded," "cut off," or "blocked," are some of the relevant Soviet expressions) in the first place by means of preemptive measures undertaken by the Soviet side.*

Helsinki Security Conference, 1975

Ever since 1965, or from the very first months of the period when Brezhnev and Kosygin were in power, Moscow sought a pan-European security conference. The conference would have several purposes. Of overriding importance were the following rationales: to translate Détente-I and Détente-II into the last stage by reducing the military potential of the West to the lowest possible point; to reduce the military, economic, and political influence of the United States on the Continent by turning West European countries eastward as well as inward; to enhance the respectability of the Soviet Union by reducing its fearsome aspect, thus abetting the respectability of Communist parties in each West European country, especially where a national party declared its independence from Moscow.

As we have seen, normalization and arrangements for détente first with France, then West Germany, and finally with the United States were all steps on the way to the all-European security conference. The conference would underwrite détente with a number of these countries, but above all, it would recognize as permanent the territorial adjustments made by the big powers during and after World War II. The conference would put the final seal, as it were, upon these settlements and thus reassure the Kremlin that the postwar frontiers, which so favored the Soviet Union in the East, were fixed and incontrovertible. This would serve to block Peking's claims since 1963 that the Soviets had unfairly acquired an empire whose unwilling subjects wished for independence.

The West Europeans put forward certain prerequisites before they agreed to the Soviet-proposed security conference, in the form of the so-called "Basket Three" discussions in Vienna. These included talks held before the conference that centered about such matters as the free exchange of information and movement of citizens between East and West. With the final wording of the

August 1, 1975, Declaration of the Conference on Security and Cooperation in Europe, it became obvious that only a partial Western victory had been achieved in the "freedom clauses" of the declaration. For what the declaration stated in effect was that any nonfulfillment of these clauses could *not* entail "direct or indirect, individual or collective, [intervention] in the internal . . . affairs falling within the domestic jurisdiction of another participating state." In terms of the Leninist aspect of Soviet foreign policy and the traditions and deeds of Cominternism and Cominformism, the following stipulation in the Helsinki Declaration is indeed curious:

> The participating states will refrain from direct or indirect assistance to terrorist activities or to subversive or other activities directed towards the violent overthrow of the regime of another participating state.

All three World Conferences of Communist and Workers' Parties (1957, 1960, and 1969) have reasserted the Leninist line— the Helsinki declaration to the contrary—that whether violent or nonviolent means are used to achieve a Socialist revolution in a capitalist country depends on the conditions prevailing in that country, most specifically, the opposition to the "inevitable" march to social progress shown by the capitalists. If the capitalists do not yield peacefully, or if they put up armed resistance to this proletarian march, violent means will have to be used, conference documents say. The Leninist tradition underlies these stipulations in international declarations by Communist parties. The influence may be traced back to several writings by Lenin in 1920, the most important of which is *The Infantile Disease of Leftwing Communism.* In this, Lenin asserted:

> History in general, and the history of revolutions in particular, teaches that history itself is far richer in content, in its variety, in its manysidedness, and is livelier and "more cunning" than even the best political parties and the most conscious members of the vanguard of the leading classes. This is understandable since the best vanguards express the consciousness, will, yearnings, and fantasies by the tens of

thousands. Meanwhile, revolution is made at moments of extraordinary upturn and tension in all human capacities involving the consciousness, will, yearnings, and fantasies of the tens of millions which are invoked by the class struggle. From this follow two important practical conclusions: first, that the revolutionary class, in carrying out its task, must be able to master *all* forms and sides of public activity, without exception (which apply no less to the post-revolutionary period than to the pre-revolutionary, both of which situations are fraught with great risks and tremendous dangers), and second, that the revolutionary class must be prepared for the swiftest and most unexpected possible exchange of one form of revolution for another.

Lenin goes on to explain in this passage that by "forms of revolution" he means violent or nonviolent means, and compares the rapid, unexpected shift from one to the other form to the tactics employed in war. He adds that the weapons used in armed violence must be of all possible types, including especially the kind "that deliver the fatal blow most rapidly," and they should be the match for any of the weapons at the disposal of the ruling classes. The switch from one form to another of revolutionary struggle, says Lenin and his followers until today, must also embrace "either legal or illegal activity"—that is, either legal or subversive activity.

The 25th Party Congress, 1976

The 25th Party Congress was the second congress held under Brezhnev and Kosygin and the latest major Soviet party airing of ideological and foreign policy issues of lasting significance. It was held between February 24 and March 3, 1976, and caused much analysis and speculation on the part of Western specialists. In the Soviet Union itself, the congress came to be considered as the "historic event" of the last half of this century. Meetings in offices, factories, and fields were held all over the country pledging support for the ideological as well as economic formulations and goals set at the congress.

In many respects, the congress turned out to be quite different from what foreign observers had expected. First, it was thought that Leonid Brezhnev, General Secretary of the Soviet Communist party, would retire or be forced out of office because of his health, advanced age, or political difficulties. Instead, Brezhnev not only amused the 4998 Soviet and foreign Communist party delegates with occasional banter between himself and a speaker at the podium, but comported himself like a supremely self-confident commissar become tsar in a marathon speech lasting five hours, with only breaks for food, drink, and other natural demands. Another line of speculation had run that the congress would feature denunciation of Communist China, just as the 20th Party Congress 20 years ago had revolved about the denunciation of Stalin. Thus, as the 20th Party Congress had gone down in history as the "de-Stalinization" conclave, the 25th Congress would be known as the "de-Sinicization" congress. But the Chinese were not denounced, and what the 25th Congress had become, in fact, was the congress of revolutionariness, revisionism and economic development.

Brezhnev introduced world revolutionariness in his address on opening day. A status quo worldwide, he said, would not prevent Communist revolutionary action. Détente actually "creates more favorable conditions" for Communism. "The Soviet Union will not interfere in the internal affairs of other countries and peoples ... *but* we do not conceal our views: In developing countries and, in fact, *everywhere,* we stand by the side of the forces of progress, democracy, and national independence toward which we respond as friends and comrades in the struggle."

Support of such struggles, said Brezhnev, are "called for by our revolutionary conscience as well as our Communist convictions." The General Secretary's report (which is customarily approved by the full membership of the ruling Politburo before it is delivered) was followed by supportive speeches by other officials. All speakers who addressed themselves to foreign affairs emphasized the traditional Leninist call for the spread of Communism by means of persuasion as well as force of arms. The gist of this updating of Lenin was that the Soviet Union would continue to pursue a "two-track" foreign policy, one adhering to conventional diplomacy, the other to a revolutionary one.

Another topic at the party congress concerned the "revisionist" trend away from traditional Leninist Communism. Most of the Communist parties throughout the world support orthodox Leninism as interpreted by Moscow, but some important "detachments" or "brigades" of Communists do not. Those that do not, especially the parties of France, Italy, and Spain, made their views known in the Kremlin Palace of Congresses at the latest congress, views that were so heretical they were edited out of the newspaper and TV reports to the Soviet people. But Soviet Politburo alternate member, Pyotr Masherov, party chief of the Byelorussian Republic, warned that no "modernization" of Marxism-Leninism will be permitted, nor will the doctrine be "cut to fit the dimensions of 'national compartments.' " One such national compartment is France, where the French Communist party won about 20 percent of the votes in cantonal elections in early March. (Municipal elections will be held in 1977 and elections for Parliament in 1978.) The French party, yielding to "Eurocommunism," decided at its own recent congress to drop the embarrassing phrase "dictatorship of the proletariat" from its party program and has criticized the Soviets for "repressions" at home.

Premier Alexei Kosygin headed the list of congress speakers who introduced and explained the new five-year economic plan. The economic goals fit rather well into the generally hard-line posture shown in the political sphere—domestic, diplomatic, and Communist party-international. First, heavy industry was to be favored over consumer goods, with one speaker frankly admitting that this priority had been set with "defense construction" in mind. Second, foreign trade and reliance on Western capitalist know-how would continue to be stressed in the years between 1976 and 1980, but at a somewhat reduced rate. Third, austerity coupled to economic development through better utilization of resources than in the past and high quality performance were keynoted. As to the possible clash between economic cooperation with the West and revolutionariness, the implication at the congress was that the West needs the trade as much as the Soviet Union, and that, in any case, the "imperialism" of the United States is becoming isolated while West European countries now do not necessarily follow Washington's orders when it comes to "holding back the inevitable processes of history" or conducting trade with the West.

Finally, the congress was almost as noteworthy for those who did not speak as it was for those who did take the rostrum. Only five out of 15 full members of the Politburo (the new body contained 16 members) spoke at the congress. Top officials like Defense Minister Marshal Andrei Grechko, Foreign Minister Andrei Gromyko, intelligence chief Yuri Andropov, and Soviet President Nikolai Podgorny kept a mysterious silence. Presumably, their silence was intended to accent the stellar performance of Brezhnev, whose "cult" has already exceeded that afforded Nikita Khrushchev, and is rapidly approaching the glorification once heaped upon Stalin. Several foreign Communist party or pro-Communist leaders absented themselves, and others left during the congress. Among these delegations were the French, whose top leader stayed home; the Egyptian leftists sent no one at all. And among those who left early were the Romanian leader, Nicolae Ceausescu, representing one of those countries and parties described by orthodox Russians and their closest allies as nationalistic and revisionistic. The concluding ceremony of singing all four verses of the "Internationale" thus contained a few sour notes.

Summary and analyses of the 25th Congress indicated a small but nevertheless marked tensing of the party line, with possible long-term consequences for Soviet foreign policy. The congress speakers, Soviet as well as foreign, imparted messages which were considerably harsher in tone when compared to the 24th "Program of Peace" Congress in 1971, or even to the 23rd Congress. While the 25th Congress explicitly updated the Program for Peace, it did so by referring to the program merely as a line laid down at the previous congress. In other words, while the 1976 Congress stated that the 1971 program was "still in effect," it emphasized internationalism far more than the peace program. This has been true, too, of post-Congress interpretations—at least up to May 1976—of the essence of the Congress reports. One such analysis, for example, appeared in *Pravda* on April 24, 1976, in the form of a book review. The book, edited by Party Secretary and ex-Comintern official Boris Ponomarev under the title, *The Workers' Movement Problems of History and Theory* (1976), was said by the reviewer, Boris Korionov, to be fully consonant with the theses of the 25th Congress. "The 25th Party Congress," observed Korionov, "noted the striking growth in influence of the

Communist parties in the capitalist countries. . . . The banner of struggle for tightening the bonds of international solidarity was hoisted still higher by the 25th CPSU Congress." The review went on to state that the workers' movement has become a crucial political factor in the world, with a strategy and tactics suited to achieving the double purpose of worldwide Socialism and world peace.

We have mentioned above, first within an ideological context and then with respect to Soviet Vietnam War policy, that Soviet diplomatic strategy since Khrushchev involved a policy of drawing the United States into a dead end (*tupik*). In fact, official statements by the Communists during and since the past war have made precisely this point. At the time of the war, with American defense expenditures largely devoted to upkeep of the anti-Communist forces in the south and bomber raids against the north, the Soviet Union and the Soviet bloc embarked on a large-scale military buildup at home. By 1970 or so, many people in the West began to surmise that American preoccupation with the war in Southeast Asia had permitted erosion of America's and NATO's defense lead over the Soviet Union while allowing major gains to be made on that lead by the Russians and their Warsaw Pact military forces. Moreover, Soviet policy-makers, with an eye to protecting their ongoing military buildup effort, strongly promoted the notion that Moscow was ready to scale down the arms race and to continue as well as to deepen détente, despite Vietnam. As the war was drawn down, so were expenditures by the United States on arms, amid tremendous domestic pressures and protests against the overweaning influence of the "military-industrial complex." This was the climate of opinion, to a large extent, under which the summits between Nixon and Brezhnev (in Moscow and Washington) and Ford and Brezhnev (in Vladivostok) were conducted. While the Soviets surely cannot take credit for the feeling against the military-industrial complex sweeping over America during and immediately after Vietnam, they surely relished and exploited it, while continuing their own virtual crash program for improving their armaments and significantly enhancing the role played by the military in Soviet schools and in civilian politics.

All this in turn was reflected in a noticeable shift in the Soviet diplomatic posture from the Vietnam policy of drawing the United States into a dilemma to a post-Vietnam War policy of confining the United States. That is to say, the Soviets had reached near parity with the United States in strategic weaponry, whether in the form of land-based missiles or sea-borne missiles. In conjunction with this, they began to describe the "worldwide correlation of forces" supporting Soviet internationalism, either with "arms in hand" (Cubans fighting in Angola) or in the form of legal and subversive political forces (Communist and pro-Communist "detachments" in capitalist countries), as having "shifted in favor of Socialism." As a result, America, and the West generally, appeared to be put under the Soviet gun. The policy of confinement, consequently, entails limiting the United States and its allies to a confined sphere of choice and of action or counteraction, well short of eliciting the danger of their triggering a third world war, or for that matter, short of their triggering or participating in a local war on the Vietnam model. Meanwhile, a confined West presumably would permit freedom of action on the part of the Soviet forces worldwide.

In conclusion, this seemed to be the message behind the several official Soviet and Soviet bloc statements of the mid-1970s that asserted that peaceful coexistence was becoming "irreversible" since it had been "forced" upon the United States and the West by Soviet strength; that no other alternative was open for the capitalist-imperialists in this new era beyond accepting peaceful coexistence and détente on Soviet terms. While perhaps seeking to avoid patently dangerous showdowns with the West on the pattern of the potentially explosive Berlin and Cuban crises of the 1960s, Soviet policymakers nevertheless seemed to be hinting, by the mid-1970s, that "next time" the Soviet side might call the American bluff, instead of the other way around. Moreover, by publicly counting its missiles for all to see, the Kremlin appeared to be advertising its military strength. This served as an accompaniment to the explicit warnings that the United States or its allies had better desist from making future, Vietnam-like "intrusions" aimed at stopping the "inevitable" tide of Communism.

So far, the response of the United States to this has taken the form of strong counterwarnings, addressed to the Soviets in 1975 and 1976 by Secretary of State Kissinger and other officials. These warnings, and other moves by the United States in the world arena, reveal an acute American awareness of the recent message issued from Moscow. Not only are the Middle East and Africa on the minds of American officials, but also Western Europe. American policy-makers seem concerned over the danger posed by a possible ultimatum posture which the Soviets might assume in some future showdown between East and West, whether over the independence of African states, the Middle East, or the safety of liberal-democratic institutions in West European countries. It remains to be seen what Washington intends to do concretely to avoid an anticipated situation in which the United States would be stymied and shut out.

*   *   *

The "look" of the second détente, in which the relationship between East and West still finds itself, has been described above in its several aspects and ramifications. It is clear that Détente-II bears a certain resemblance to Détente-I, both as to motivation and underlying ideology. Just as with the first détente, the Kremlin in the second has been motivated to pursue less tense relations with Western Europe and America. For one thing, the going from crisis to crisis, often in the face of Soviet obduracy, only raised fears in the West of the "Soviet menace." This in turn tended to militate against Soviet interests by seriously detracting from Soviet respectability, thus harming Soviet diplomacy in the West as well as the standing of pro-Soviet Communist parties and their allies in Western elections; playing a major role in inducing the Western nations to spend more on defense while welding together more tightly the member countries of NATO; and creating crises, which in the thermonuclear age and in the presence of girded-up, highly prepared military establishments in Western and in Eastern Europe, would become perhaps too hot to handle, at least if the crises arose within the main European theater.

The second détente under Brezhnev extends to a variety of issues in a way in which all previous respites in confrontations between East and West have not. These issues include arms limitations, trade between East and West, and an evolving process of political summitry which could have even greater importance in the years ahead than it already has up to now. Also, the problem Russia is having with China, which has a great bearing upon its relations with the West, loomed larger during the time of the second détente than in the first (see next chapter, pp. 171-174), especially as the result of Mao's death in September 1976.

In the next chapter, by way of concluding the book, we will assess further the military, economic, and political results of the policy of détente. This assessment includes a calculation of the prospects for deepening détente, based on the achievements to date towards securing détente, while taking into account the latest trends.

6

The Prospects for Deepening Détente

From Lenin to Brezhnev, the Soviet rulers have claimed that by following the "compass of Marxism-Leninism," their policies have been based upon supreme wisdom, science, and political art, and that they have been outstanding for their realism. The Soviet record over the past 60 years shows that the regime in Moscow *has* exhibited more cautiousness than recklessness, more deliberation than impetuousness, more rationality than irrationality. Because of this, the totalitarian dictatorship in Russia can be said to display a good deal more circumspection and predictability than the dictatorships in Fascist Italy and Nazi Germany. The first totalitarian regime, after all, has outlived all the others, and this fact undoubtedly testifies to Moscow's cautiousness and prudence.

And yet the Soviet regime flirts with danger, as it has from the very beginning. It invented, in fact, the form of brinkmanship represented by the policy of "neither peace nor war," a phrase and a policy conceived in the Kremlin. While they shun unreasonable risks, the Soviets nevertheless take calculated risks, especially when the armed forces and territories of others are involved, as in Korea, Vietnam, Angola, the Congo, and elsewhere. The risks, even if "calculated," remain a dangerous liability in the age of thermonuclear weapons.

More important than the risks Moscow has taken are the ideological underpinnings for these actions which inspire and guide the major policies and actions of the Soviet Union. And while weapons technology has had some influence on it, this ideology in its most important essentials remains changeless and immovable. It is still possible that this anachronistic pursuit of worldwide revolution and dominion ultimately will drive the world into global conflict and catastrophe.

War and Peace and Détente

Both détentes were formed in the midst of the danger of war on a large scale. Détente still is buoyed up by this threat, for the very powers that initiated and led in the process of relaxing tension, the Soviet Union and the United States, are the world's mightiest superpowers, the states that would suffer the most destruction of lives and property in such a war, also the states most likely to initiate or be the principal participants in the holocaust.

During the nearly 35 years since the end of World War II, the world has been a most unquiet place, and the superpowers have been deeply involved, although not always directly so, in this disquiet. Some 15 major military conflicts have occurred in this era of "peace." There have been more than 150 uprisings, riots, and violent revolutions which have involved 40 countries and two-thirds of the world's population. In reviewing these grim statistics, a spokesman in the Communist world openly admitted that the "main proponents in all these wars and armed conflicts were the progressive social forces acting as the standard-bearers" *(Borba* [Yugoslavia], May 14, 1976). In addition to the major conflicts there have been various "brush-fire conflicts." In all, there have been a total of 164 various small and large wars, most of which have involved the motif of "class-struggle."

It is clear that the problem of war and peace dwarfs all the other problems, whether concerning trade, ecology, energy resources, communications, cultural exchange, food, or travel. The preparations for war only add to the other problems in the world, for expenditures on defense entail an enormous drainage of revenues and natural resources, especially on the part of the "northern" industrialized countries of Eastern and Western Europe and North America ($200 billion). But it is precisely these countries who, if they moved in concert and unison toward solving the world's human problems, would be the most effective agents in making our planet a safer and more tranquil place. Should the powers not only fail to move together to solve the problems, but, worse, drift backwards into some new form of international tension potentially far more lethal than the tensions of the 1940s and 1950s, the resulting climate would utterly disrupt what solid ground exists today for starting to build "positive coexistence," or mutually profitable as well as mutually trustworthy relations.

Here, propaganda has a strong influence upon tension and upon nations' reactions to these tensions. In part, the decisions that the nations make in order to protect themselves, or to eliminate the supposed or actual threat to their existence, depend on how they perceive the global political programs and pretensions of others. When Communist spokesmen in the Soviet bloc declare openly that might of arms is directly related to the justness of their cause (as implied by the statement that the "correlation of forces is shifting in the Socialist favor" is the basic determiner of world history), their militant language cannot help but generate fear—fear even within the Socialist camp itself.

For example, the Yugoslav military commentator, Dimitrije Seserinac, reacted by attacking the East German Defense Minister, General Heinz Hoffmann, for his endorsement last April in the East Berlin publication, *Einheit,* of relying on the military, including a nuclear World War III, to reach Socialism. To expand a bit on Mr. Seserinac's first published criticism of the general: The *Borba* military commentator disputed the Soviet Bloc general's view that a third world war would merely constitute a "continuation of politics by other [military] means." Such a war, countered the Yugoslav, cannot be considered a "continuation of the policy of class struggle," he wrote, "but 'merely' the destruction of the world!" Seserinac further disputed General Hoffmann's adherence to the Soviet politico-military party line that the West is preparing a nuclear war for capitalism and for the destruction of Socialism. The West is not preparing such a war, insisted Seserinac, so how can the East prepare for it?

Seserinac continued:

[The role of the Soviet Union and the Bloc] cannot be to destroy the imperialist and reactionary forces in a "general, just nuclear war" in order to make it possible for all the progressive forces in the world to seize power from the hands of the exploiters. Moreover, the adoption of such a role by the Socialist countries would suit the world's imperialist and neo-colonialist forces. As is well known, these forces do not lag behind in technology, either in general or in matters of armaments. They are ready to spend money when their armed forces are in question. By implementing their threat to turn a nuclear war into one of general destruction, they could postpone indefinitely any solution of the burning socio-economic problems in countries fighting for their independence and freedom—that is, if those countries wait for the armed forces of the Socialist Bloc countries to solve all their problems by means of a new war.

Strong words by the Yugoslav journalist, who was clearly following orders from higher up in Belgrade. So as to make the Yugoslav rebuttal clearer, Mr. Seserinac returned to the attack three days later, again taking the same Warsaw Pact general to task in the pages of the party newspaper *Borba*. He reiterated one of the points of his first article:

[The facts] argue against [General Hoffmann's] thesis that the NATO countries are preparing a nuclear war against the Soviet Union and the Warsaw Pact states . . . It is also difficult to conceive what interests the citizens, workers, and peasants in the Warsaw Pact countries would have in waging a war against West Germany, France, Italy, the Netherlands, and other countries. . . . That is why the third thesis advanced by the author in the East Berlin periodical *Einheit* is untenable. Namely, the thesis that Central Europe has become, for the United States and world imperialism, the most important area in their march against Socialism. The reason is very simple: The claim that the U.S. . . . is preparing for a nuclear settling of accounts with the Soviet Union and the Warsaw

Pact countries has, as already mentioned, no foundation whatsoever.

Then the Yugoslav columnist made this distinction between the "class-struggle" origins of a third world war and the consequences such a war would have for those same proletarian classes which would presumably "profit" from it:

> [General Hoffmann's thesis] contradicts the views on just wars held by Marx and Lenin. Both of them maintained that the justness of a given war depended not solely on the reasons for which it was launched, but also on the *results* and *consequences* it brought about. If we take as a starting point that a future world war would inevitably become a nuclear war—i.e., a war of total destruction—then, we must ask, What consequences would such a war bring about?

Mr. Seserinac appears to be alone among Communist spokesmen as opposed to the notion that might makes right, whether the might takes the form of nukes or automatic rifles. That political power grows out of the barrel of a gun was not a maxim invented by Mao Tse-tung; it is at least as old as Thracymachus and Machiavelli, von Treitschke, and the more militant Marxists such as Lenin. Today, violence is tailored into the idea of class struggle, national-liberation struggle, and the "final destruction of capitalism in a third world war." Pacifists are naïve, asserted Lenin, if they think that peace can be achieved—as long as capitalism exists anywhere in the world—without resort to arms. Is this not contradictory—fighting fire with fire, or war in the name of peace? No, say the Leninists, it is the dialectical way of looking at the problem of war and peace.

Brezhnev is the latest Marxist-Leninist dialectician. On the question of war and peace, Marshal Brezhnev borrowed from the heritages of both Lenin and Stalin, but he has also added some of his own ideas. In the foregoing chapters, we have given an account of these Brezhnev emendations to Leninism and Stalinism in the area of foreign policy (especially détente) and politico-military doctrine and strategy. His contributions have mostly revolved about the use or the threat of the use of force. And he has used the promise of continued relaxation of tension, not as mere propaganda to offset the stern pronouncements on revolution, national liberation, and armed violence, but more as a *subtle form of ultimatum.*

That is, when spokesmen for the Brezhnev regime assert that there "can be no alternative to détente," or that "détente has become irreversible," they back up the statement with the strongly implied warning that the Soviets will not *permit* retreats from the policy of détente between East and West, as they define those retreats. This in turn is connected to the notion that certain rules of international politics apply to peaceful coexistence and détente, as the Soviets conceive them. As we have shown above, such "rules" condone the practice of national-liberation struggle while at the same time they condemn any "capitalist, imperialist interference with the forward march of the peoples toward social progress" as "imperialist reaction" and the "export of counter-revolution," both of which must be overcome with arms. As we have also seen above, Mr. Brezhnev himself explained this Soviet interpretation of "noninterference in the affairs of other countries and peoples" in a section of his report to the 25th Party Congress in February 1976. His explanation was evidently so significant and crucial that it was repeated almost word for word in two successive book reviews written for *Pravda* and *Izvestia* by the papers' chief foreign affairs editors. One of these reiterations of the Brezhnev line went as follows *(Izvestia,* April 3, 1976):

Our country does not interfere in the internal affairs of other countries and peoples. *But* we do not conceal our views. In the developing countries, as everywhere else, we stand by the side of the forces of progress, democracy and national independence.

George Orwell, if he had been able to read the above quotation before he wrote *1984,* would probably have used it as an illustration of "doublethink." For *Izvestia's* gloss on the Brezhnev statement to the party congress contains those same characteristic utterances made by Lenin, Stalin, Khrushchev, and Brezhnev. That is, the Russians say that nations cannot interfere in the affairs of other nations or "peoples," meaning by the latter forces not yet organized into nations but merely into bands of guerrillas, or "patriotic forces." *"But,"* we Soviets can interfere—if the forces of progress, democracy and national independence demand our armed support. In another part of his congress address, Brezhnev said that he and his colleagues would follow their "revolutionary conscience" when making decisions concerning other states and peoples.

As Soviet military power has sharply increased over the past dozen years, Brezhnev also has introduced the notion that the Leninist formulation of the correlation of class forces may now be extended globally. Moreover, the "forces" are no longer vaguely defined expressions of class solidarity, support for the peace movement, or general strikes, but are regarded as tangible military force. One Soviet spokesman declares that "our army is facilitating the people's struggle for social progress" while another maintains that the Soviet bloc's approach to military parity with the West is the "essential condition and guarantee for the most successful forward movement of the world revolutionary process." Thus, the "correlation of forces," as well as détente, harbors a threat to world peace.

Whether or not détente will develop into a lasting and constructive partnership between the largest nations of the world depends, of course, on whether or not the East—or at least the Soviet segment of it—continues to produce militant tracts such as *Marxism-Leninism on War and Army* or *The Philosophical Heritage of V. I. Lenin and Problems of Contemporary War.* That is, the alarming ideas contained in their pages also will contribute to the spread of mistrust and suspicion among the great powers. Détente, relaxation of tension, thus becomes frustrated by the tension and concern over Soviet and Communist revolutionism and the Soviet double standard of following the revolutionary conscience above the law among nations while insisting that the capitalist states strictly obey *both* sets of rules—the traditional, "bourgeois" ones as well as the rules of the game laid down by the Communists.

War, Arthur Koestler wrote recently, is not fought today for territory per se as much as it is for "words in semantic space." It is motivated, he said, "not by aggression nor by territory, but by love." This is the kind of "love," in quotation marks, that led Lenin to say that people must be hit over the head to see the truth, to realize a way of life containing higher, more humanitarian and altruistic standards than the life of non-Communists and capitalists; a reforming zeal and a conviction that the old world is dying and that a new world waits to take its place. Love, not hatred; "self-transcending devotion" (Koestler), not unmitigated scorn, seem to propel Communist ideology and Communist leaders personally into further violent acts "in the name of all mankind."

Meanwhile, the outlook remains bleak that Communist leadership will ever disown Marxism-Leninism or forsake what Stalin called the revolutionary "Vow to Lenin." This vow has been renewed by Communist leaders of the Soviet bloc since the promise was first made in 1924. "Ideological disarmament" will never occur on the Communist side, Soviet spokesmen have emphasized. They recently reemphasized this when they were challenged on the point by such Western statesmen as President Giscard of France and Prime Minister Fraser of Australia.

So far as war and peace are concerned, all the policies, of enforcing détente and revolutionism, leave the "objects" of the Communist zealots' affection and devotion only one choice: to arm themselves in their own defense. But the West and its friends must do something more than merely defend themselves. What is called the "Western way of life" must rededicate itself to its own best convictions, while each country must strengthen itself in the moral sense, as well as in the economic and material sense. As each link in the chain of Western nations is strengthened, the whole chain becomes more resistant to internal and external threats to its existence. "Our *first* priority," Zbigniew Brzezinski asserted to the Democratic party platform committee in the spring of 1976, "must be to create more stable and cooperative relations among the advanced industrialized democracies of North America, Western Europe, and the Far East."

Western resolve to strengthen its policies, in both the spiritual and material senses, depends largely on the will, intellect and imagination of its peoples and leaders. And these three special functions of mankind have by no means been neglected by Western nations in the past, throughout the history of Western civilization. But at present, there are the counterproductive phenomena of flaccidity, of continuing in the old way, or becoming "soft" and distracted by the pursuit of material pleasure to the extreme of mass self-indulgence, none of which is conducive to girding up and integrating the separate nations. With perhaps crueler irony and perspicacity than even he himself imagined that he possessed, the Soviet premier who assumed power immediately after Stalin died, Georgi Malenkov, made this incisive remark in his inaugural address in 1953:

> If today, under conditions of tension in relations, the North Atlantic bloc is rent by internal strife and contradictions, the lessening of this tension may lead to its disintegration.

It is clear enough from what Malenkov openly stated, and from the policies that have been developed and pursued in the Kremlin since 1953, that the Soviet leadership sees in détente a means whereby the Western nations may be induced to slacken their efforts to strengthen themselves and their relations with each other.

So far, "Western disintegration" or decline has not occurred, nor is there any indication that it will in the foreseeable future. While economic or political difficulties surely do exist in Italy, the Iberian Peninsula, Latin America, among other places, Western resolve over its military defenses has not waned significantly. Member countries of NATO, for instance, have not decelerated their defense programs to any significant degree during the détente years. But Western strength must be measured above all in social, political, psycho-social, and cultural terms. Here one finds, as many have pointed out within the Western countries themselves, a somewhat ambiguous picture. One sees people bent upon material indulgence and individualism coupled to a tolerance or indifference to the dangers to their way of life that the indulgence poses, as well as to the external threat posed by the Marxist-Leninist bid for a totalitarian way of life which is "communal" and regimented, planned and unexciting. The Soviet bloc must presently be assessed as potentially the stronger of the two worlds. It is better equipped to impose its way of life on others than others are on it. Consequently, "world power assessments" continually attribute the Soviet bloc strength to a tightly controlled population which is compelled to undergo paramilitary training at the grade-school level and indoctrinated with a moral upbringing which buttresses the national purpose, and multiplies the brute power the Russians can project into the international arena.

The Record

Chapters 2 through 5 reviewed the Soviet historical record with regard to the efforts the Russians have made to attain peaceful coexistence and relaxation of tension. The record is strewn with what one observer of Soviet foreign policy has called "promises and pitfalls." Unfortunately, the pitfalls outweigh the promises.

From the time of its Leninist inception in the form of "peaceful cohabitation" in the early 1920s, coexistence between East and West has been understood and presented doctrinally by the Russians as a sometime thing. Lenin stressed the temporariness of the connection. Moreover, Lenin conceived of the relationship mainly in terms of the preservation of the Soviet state, as a means whereby the West could be distracted from interfering in Soviet affairs—domestic as well as foreign. After the preservation and protection of the Soviet Republic from any future foreign "intervention," the second priority, according to Lenin, went to the preservation and strengthening of the Soviet "base" to prepare for world revolution and the establishment of a Soviet Republic of the Whole World. Without a strong center, in terms of both leadership and economic and military strength, the Russian-led march of world revolution would become a mere idealist's fantasy, lacking realistic underpinnings. However, he promulgated a policy of "retreat" to gain economic strength, which he saw as an indispensable prerequisite for political, revolutionary, and military strength. But Lenin died precisely at the time when his new policies of taking one step backward to prepare for two steps forward was just getting underway. It is impossible to say when Lenin, had he lived, would have terminated the retreat, and reopened the offensive for Socialism, both at home and abroad.

Stalin contended that Lenin's true behest had been that the Socialist offensive on the home front should be mounted immediately. He also felt the offensive should be taken because he saw an approaching era of capitalist decline and an invitation to wage a revolutionary offensive on the foreign front. Coming as the prediction did just before the outbreak of the Great Depression, Stalin's prognosis about the wretched state of Western capitalism at that time was on target. So was his prediction of the coming of a colossal "inter-imperialist" war—to which prediction he had been automatically led, as it were, by his Leninist premises concerning imperialism. To call the war "inter-imperialist" was a misnomer, of course, but Stalin formulated most of his world assessments in ideological terms, as do his successors. And he accordingly ordered Communist fifth columns in the capitalist nations to prepare "proletarian" takeovers. Stalin maintained that

> The most important results of the world economic crisis are to uncover and aggravate the contradictions inherent in world capitalism.... A revolutionary crisis is ripening and will continue to ripen.

Again, he said that aid rendered by the first Socialist country should be expressed by the fact that, first, the

> victorious proletariat ... after organizing its own Socialist production, should stand up ... *against* the remaining, capitalist world, attracting to itself the oppressed classes of other countries, raising revolts in those countries against the capitalists, and in the event of necessity, coming out even with armed force against the exploiting classes and their governments.

So obsessed, in fact, was Stalin with revolutionism, and subversion in the capitalist world, that his government totally underestimated the danger to world peace presented by Italian and German Fascism, both of which Stalin at first considered to be minor threats by "moribund capitalism." But along with this underestimation, Stalin refused to reach agreement with the Western powers on how to stop Hitler and Mussolini. The results are well known.

In the light of reading the various writings published during the Brezhnev period, it becomes obvious that this Stalinist record of a stubborn pursuit of Leninist revolution on the one hand and the seeking for an advantage in international relations at Western expense on the other remains unexamined and uncriticized in *Soviet* historiography. And this fact is not only of historiographic interest. It is vitally pertinent to the present existence of détente, to the durability of détente, and its conversion into truly positive, cooperative coexistence. For what the Brezhnev materials continue to maintain in effect is that both Lenin and Stalin were right in pursuing their short-sighted, autarkic, Russia-first foreign policies coupled to the Comintern tactic of disuniting the West wherever possible and giving encouragement and tangible support to subversive elements in capitalist countries.

The Russians, their setbacks notwithstanding, continue to pursue Leninist revolution and the advantage it may give in international relations at the expense of the West. And even though the Soviets in the 1970s entered into the SALT-I talks, summit meetings, the Helsinki accords, and treaties affecting trade, communications, and cultural exchange, they also paid greater attention than they had before to the military. Meanwhile, they stressed the following ideological positions:

• The rebirth of Leninist Cominternism, and recollection of the 57-year heritage of the Third Communist International.
• Soviet rededication to the more violent aspects contained in Marxism-Leninism on war and the use of force.
• The birth of some particularly Brezhnevist doctrines concerning correlation of forces, irreversibility of detente, the approaching last stage in the decline of capitalism, the use of the offensive in politics and military art, among others.
• Strong efforts to regroup the world's Communists around the Moscow center, with very dubious success.
• Diplomatic and inter-CP efforts to isolate the Chinese from the rest of the world and ostracize them from the "Socialist camp."
• Many-sided effort to isolate and "hem in" the United States as the bastion of world imperialism.

In pondering these phenomena in the historical record of Detente-II, one should not ignore the positive features:

• Greatly increased East-West commerce (three times that

of 1970), although with the prospect that not much more room exists for increasing it further in the years ahead, at least not at the impressive rate of the early 1970s.

• Increased diplomatic intercourse between the nations of the East and West marked by summit talks and the work of foreign-affairs special committees and commissions in areas of mutual concern to the countries (problems relating to environment, the World Ocean, trade, cultural exchange, attempts to control sales of nuclear materials and other equipment).

• Contact and mutual consultation on the matter of threats to the nations' security and the preventive measures to be undertaken, should a crisis arise and threaten the peace between the major powers. And other positive features could be added to the list.

In weighing the pluses against the minuses, one is led to this tentative conclusion: The second détente, evolving since 1969, does bear traces of significant departures from its Khrushchev-Stalin-Lenin predecessors. But the departures lead in two directions—one favorable, the other unfavorable. Meanwhile, the unfavorable elements pose far more dangers than was true in any of the preceding relaxations in the history of East-West relations.

The fact that the Russians have been willing to enter summit talks and to agree to treaties seemingly increases the possibility that détente will succeed. But that the Russians pursue the old-line policies as well makes the success of détente less likely.

The Present Look of Détente

There have been certain hopeful signs, since the spring of 1976, that the second détente may have a longer life than was originally thought and that recent developments within the Kremlin may serve to improve relations between the East and West. Most important, perhaps, is the fact that Mr. Brezhnev's health is widely believed to incapacitate him from exercising complete power in the Kremlin. Whether Brezhnev retires, is forced out, or dies, candidates who appear to be more moderate wait to take over. The trend towards more moderate policies was indicated when a civilian was made the Minister of Defense after Marshal Grechko died and the military lost a seat on the Politburo. Then Foreign Minister Gromyko travelled to Britain and France to stress the "deepening of détente." And the Soviet press began to appeal for congresses with the West on economic, environmental, energy, and other matters of mutual concern (perhaps to avoid energy crises and inflation in Russia as well as to improve peaceful coexistence). This, the Russian press suggested, might be done by improving cooperation between the Common Market and the "Communist Market" (COMECON), and by more commerce with the West.

The Soviets also have indicated that they repudiate Lenin's notion of the merely temporary nature of their relationship with the West. They also have deemphasized the militant tone of Marxism-Leninism in favor of a campaign to collect signatures for peace (first carried out in the 1950 Stockholm Peace Appeal, but which was followed by the Korean War and the cold war, and seemed to be only a disguise for Communist aggression).

Most important, perhaps, the Russians have given approval, in Berlin, early in the summer of 1976, to centrifugality or polycentrism within the European Communist movement. This may help détente, not only because the concession would weaken the strength of the Soviet Bloc to some extent, but because it gives each nation in the bloc more freedom to design its own domestic and foreign strategies, unrestrained from the rigors of internationalism as interpreted by Moscow. This, in turn, could induce the Russians to follow a more flexible foreign policy as well. In addition, Communist parties in foreign countries were given greater freedom to follow different roads in the struggle for social change. The June 1976 document constituted a new precedent which will be difficult for the Soviets to violate or undo. In fact, the price paid for any future violation could turn out to be disastrous for the Communist movement. The movement would become fractionalized beyond recall, splitting up into independent, pro-Soviet, or Maoist factions.

Further consequences flowing from the East Berlin agreement affect the internal affairs of West European countries, and, along with them, détente. This stems from the possibility that, by loosening their bonds to the more orthodox Soviet party, the

Western Communists may win voter support within the electorates of the democratic countries. This could lead to Communist participation in one or several of the coalition regimes emerging from future elections in Western Europe. Since the national Communist parties insist that they are becoming increasingly committed to strictly national goals and programs in the Western democracies, Western Communist parties might become more supportive of traditional Western foreign-policy positions, up to and including vigilance on the global designs of Russia. (The East Berlin document makes mention of "hegemonism" as a danger to world peace, and it is by no means clear whether the hegemonism is Soviet or Chinese, or both.) At least one of the parties, the Italian Communist party, has already indicated that it will support Italy's continuing participation in the NATO alliance. The French party, in the person of its leader, Georges Marchais, made reference at its most recent party congress to Soviet "repressions" within the Soviet Union and to the necessity of holding high a form of strictly French Communism. While this party still supports the Gaullist policy that France should go it alone as far as Atlanticism is concerned, it has nevertheless had to back away from orthodox Gaullism, after President Giscard gradually began to steer the country back into the Atlantic fold; the French are now far more cooperative with the NATO countries, in the military context, than in past years.

Whether or not any Western Communist parties actually do acquire power or even participate in Western governments in the future, the effect of the polycentrism of Western Communist parties on relations between East and West is bound to be healthy.

The Chinese in the Future of Détente

Although Mao's troops had not been sent out of China since the days of the Korean War and the occupation of Tibet, and had been involved only in border skirmishes with the Indians in 1962, and with the Soviets in 1969, and at other times, their credo on war and peace is no less sanguinary than that of the militants in the Kremlin. Mao (or his successors) never retracted, so far as is known, his famous assertion in 1957 that hundreds of millions of victims of a third world war would be worth it if capitalism were finally destroyed and Socialism put in its place. But the Maoist regime was also one of the first Communist states to propound peaceful coexistence in the post-Stalin period, at the Bandung Conference of 1955. So, peaceful coexistence *and* militant revolutionism are regarded by the Chinese (as they are by the Leninists) as a "dialectical combination of opposites."

Moreover, for years, Peking has been trying to upstage the Soviets on the matter of correctly interpreting peaceful coexistence and détente and adjusting it to the doctrines of Marxism-Leninism. In one such effort in the mid-1960s, entitled "Peaceful Coexistence—Two Diametrically Opposed Policies," the Chinese accused the "Khrushchevites" in the Kremlin of distorting Leninism and its teaching on peaceful coexistence. This article, reproduced in *Red Flag,* quotes from Lenin's writings that it claims have somehow been "overlooked" by theoreticians in Moscow, who now choose, instead, more innocuous utterances and make glosses that harmonize better with the moderate aspects of Brezhnevist détente. The Chinese, for example, pointed to Lenin's statement of July 28, 1920, that the forerunner of the United Nations, the League of Nations, was an essentially imperialist club, outside of which the "revolutionary struggle is everywhere intensifying ... accelerating the destruction of petty-bourgeois national illusions about the possibility of peaceful coexistence ... under capitalism."

Red Flag also reproduced the Lenin statement on the Draft Program of the Russian Communist party to the effect that the "party's foreign policy [consists of] rendering support to the revolutionary movement of the Socialist proletariat in the advanced countries [and] of the democratic and revolutionary movement in all countries in general, and particularly in the colonies and dependent countries." And, finally, one of the most brutal "scientific predictions" ever made by Lenin was recalled by the Chinese party journal: "The existence of the Soviet Republic side by side with imperialist states for a long time is unthinkable. One or the other must triumph in the end. And before that end supervenes, a series of frightful collisions between the Soviet Republic and the bourgeois states will be inevitable."

Interestingly, in the 1970s, especially since Red China's admission into the United Nations and the Sino-American démarche signaled by President Nixon's visit to Peking in 1972, the Chinese have concentrated their criticism upon *Soviet* militancy, and the Brezhnev "militarist" program; they are likely to continue in this way in the aftermath of Mao's death.

In a pamphlet published in Peking in 1974, under the title "Cheap Propaganda," the Chinese news agency accused Moscow of making "fraudulent" disarmament proposals and of using détente as a mask for planning Soviet military expansion. A quotation from Lenin is reproduced in order to embarrass the Kremlin for not making an honest effort to scale down preparations for war: "We should like to see a minimum of general assurances, solemn promises, and grandiloquent formulas," said Lenin, "and the greatest possible number of the simplest and most obvious decisions and measures that would definitely lead to peace." Even so, the Chinese continue to build up their own military forces. And, as remarked above, they have never revised the militancy of Maoism on the question of the forcible spread of Socialism on a global scale. More recently the situation has developed in which China looks to the West for support because the Chinese feel they are in danger of being invaded by the Russians. (The Chinese have even encouraged the West to strengthen NATO as a block to Soviet expansion.) Clearly all sides should gain if the Chinese normalize their relations with foreign countries, including the Soviet Union.

If Vietnam represented a way in which Sino-Soviet rivalry and animosity within the Communist world could seriously aggravate tensions, inability or unwillingness on the part of the Chinese and Russians to find new Vietnams in which to play out their hostility or show their fidelity to revolutionism would also help spread and deepen détente. But has the Vietnam-type of Sino-Soviet rivalry ended? Already, North Korea seems to be the focal point of a new and potentially dangerous outbreak of Sino-Soviet competition, and of world tension. Both Moscow and Peking are attempting to win the friendship of the Kim Il Sung regime in Pyongyang by promising support for Kim's effort to "peacefully unify the North and the South." The same expression was used in the case of Vietnam; the country's "peaceful unification" was said to have been in the process of realization precisely when the Communist forces showed the most aggressiveness and the war peaked in ferocity. Should Korea become the new battleground for testing Soviet and Chinese revolutionism, the United States and its allies would be seriously challenged, and East-West détente seriously impaired, if not destroyed altogether. The ensuing situation would be fraught with far more danger than the war in Vietnam. This war occurred, after all, before the Brezhnev regime had completed (and advertised, through SALT-I) the enormous military buildup, which still (in 1976) consumes upwards to 15% of Soviet G.N.P., as contrasted to the American defense expenditures at less than half this percentage.

What Is To Be Done?

Until very recently, the Brezhnev ideology of détente has not boded well for the future of détente. (Even with the recent developments pointing toward moderation of Soviet policy along several lines that may affect détente in a favorable way, the Soviet Union must continue to be regarded as a most dangerous adversary. Until the Russians make a major ideological revision in Marxism-Leninism, détente will continue to be regarded by Moscow, as we have seen, as a means of conducting its campaign to control or at least strongly influence key areas of the globe while strengthening its economy by means of taking advantage of trade with the West and borrowing Western technology and industrial know-how. Coupled to its on-going arms buildup, the militant ideology of Soviet Marxism-Leninism will continue to possess more than academic interest and prove to be a good deal more than a mere bluff.)Certainly, the Soviet Union deserves to be carefully watched and tested in the months and years ahead. A possibly favorable development for the future success of détente might be the coming to power in the United States of a new administration under President Carter. Among Carter's foreign-policy advisers will undoubtedly continue to be George Ball and Zbigniew Brzezinski, two veteran foreign-affairs specialists known for their flexibility of mind and imagination. These are precisely the qualities that are necessary in dealing with the Soviets at a time when the Kremlin itself faces some momentous choices as to successors to the many aging leaders within today's Politburo, among whom are Suslov, Podgorny, Kosygin, and Pel'she, and Mr. Brezhnev himself. And the new efforts with respect to the Soviet Union, the Soviet bloc, and détente, could quite possibly lead to:

• Encouragement of the "deepening-of-détente" line ushered in by the USSR after April 1976.
• Reconvening of the Geneva Conference on the Middle East, possibly resulting in superpower cooperation in forestalling another war in the region.
• Tangible upgrading of pan-European cooperation in the form of cooperation on energy resources and commerce, and greater cultural, tourist, and other intercourse.
• Relaxation on the domestic front in many of the bloc countries, which many expected to ensue after the Helsinki conference, as a windfall of détente between the East and West—especially if an event such as the Polish food riots of spring 1976 or other public protests should push Communist regimes into further liberalization, as they did to some extent in 1953, 1956, and 1970 (years of unrest, respectively, in East Germany, Poland and Hungary, and a second time in Poland).
• Further aggravation of Sino-Soviet relations may not be automatically favorable for détente, since the repercussions from Sino-Soviet tension could prove to be ultimately explosive. Nevertheless the quality of these relations could be a factor that encourages Soviet attention to its Western rear and which urges it into closer ties with the West (the second détente was undoubtedly encouraged by the Sino-Soviet border clashes of that year).

* * *

A new administration in Washington—or a reelected one—that combined forthrightness with imagination, cool diplomacy with a sense of moral purpose, could find a United States that was not only rising to its former heights of influence in world affairs but even earning some new-found respect throughout the world. Above all, wisdom coupled to what Plato called "rational courage" will be a mighty determiner of how well the United

States begins its tricentennial in foreign relations. It may prove necessary for the United States to take a stronger stance than hitherto on the Soviets' and their allies' following of their "revolutionary conscience." Indeed, future Vietnams, Angolas, or Koreas would have to be prevented, or the world will continue to witness more such conflicts. In fact, a stronger stance than formerly will have to be taken by America and its allies on a whole range of violent actions that continue throughout the world—whether in the form of political kidnappings, assassinations, hijackings, or other forms of extortion; outright "national-liberation war," or domestic unrest and violence instigated by left-wing forces in the democracies. The Yugoslav military commentator, Dimitrije Seserinac, was correct when he pointed out that most of the violence during the post-World War II era had been instigated by Marxist-Leninists. What he did not note was that Western acquiescence to some of this violence not only has not prevented its spread, but has probably abetted it. It is time, also, to link up Communist behavior with Communist acquisition of Western technology, and of Soviet acquisition of American grain. While it may have been improper for a rider to have been placed on bestowing Most Favored Nation Status upon the Soviet Union (the Jackson-Vanik amendment requiring the Soviet Union to ease emigration restrictions in the Soviet Union), it is *distinctly not improper for the West to make demands on the East that affect international tranquility.* The most important Western demands should become the price for the most vitally-needed Western commodities by the East.

These are some of the problems confronting the leadership in Washington as it draws various conclusions from reviews of the record of the past seven years of détente. A new feeling of strength and a sense of national unity and purpose, already in evidence in the United States on the double occasion of its 200th birthday and the anticipated election of a promising President, will do much to assure the success of détente, or in preventing détente from serving as a mere charade or blind for making the world safe for Communism. A show of American and allied fortitude could have positive results for peace and for the future of the world:

"Fortes fortuna adjuvat." *

---

* "Fortune smiles on those who show courage."—Terence.

Bibliography

Aleksandrov, V. V., et al. *Mezhdunarodnoye Kommunisticheskoye, Rabocheye i Natsional'no-Osvoboditel'noye Dvizheniye. Uchebnoye Posobiye. (International Communist, Workers', and National-Liberation Movement. School Textbook.)* Higher Party School Attached to the CPSU Central Committee, "Mysl'," Moscow, 1974, Part II, 1939-1973.

Brezhnev, L. I. *Leninskii Kurs. Rechi i Stat'i (The Lenin Course. Speeches and Articles),* Izdatel'stvo Politicheskoi Literatury, Moscow, 1970-1976, 5 vols.

———. *O Vneshnei Politike KPSS i Sovetskovo Gosudarstva. Rechi i Stat'i (On the Foreign Policy of the CPSU and the Soviet State. Speeches and Articles),* Izdatel'stvo Politicheskoi Literatury, Moscow, 1975.

Butenko, A. P., et al. *Sotsializm i Mezhdunarodniye Otnosheniya (Socialism and International Relations),* Izdatel'stvo "Nauka," Moscow, 1975.

Chubaryan, A. O. *V. I. Lenin i Formirovaniye Sovetskoi Vneshnei Politiki (V. I. Lenin and the Formation of Soviet Foreign Policy),* Izdatel'stvo "Nauka," Moscow, 1972.

Degras, Jane (ed.). *The Communist International, 1919-1943:*

Documents, Oxford University Press, London, 1956-1960, Vols. 1-2.

Grechko, A. A. *Vooruzhenniye Sily Sovetskovo Gosudarstva (The Armed Forces of the Soviet State),* Voennoye Izdatel'stvo Ministerstva Oborony SSSR, 2nd ed., Moscow, 1975.

Gromyko, A. A. and Ponomarev, B. N. (eds). *Istoriya Vneshnei Politiki SSSR, 1917-1975, v Dvukh Tomakh (History of the Foreign Policy of the USSR, 1917-1975, in Two Volumes),* Izdatel'stvo "Nauka," Moscow, 1976.

Khrushchev, N. S. (Edward Crankshaw, ed.). *Khrushchev Remembers,* Little, Brown and Company, Boston, 1970.

———. (Strobe Talbott, ed.). *Khrushchev Remembers The Last Testament,* Little, Brown and Company, Boston, 1974.

V. I. Lenin i Vneshnyaya Politika Sotsialisticheskovo Gosudarstva. Sbornik Statei Istorikov Kievskovo Ordena Lenina Gosudarstvennovo Universiteta (V. I. Lenin and the Foreign Policy of the Soviet State. Collection of Articles by Historians of the Kiev Order of Lenin State University), Izdatel'stvo Kievskovo Universiteta, Kiev, 1972.

Lenin on the United States. Selections from the Writings of V. I. Lenin, International Publishers, New York, 1970.

Lenin, V. I. *Polnoye Sobraniye Sochinenii (Collected Works),* Izdatel'stvo Politicheskoi Literatury, Moscow, 1960-, 55 vols.

Marxism-Leninism on War and Army, Progress Publishers, Moscow, 1972.

Milovidov, A. S. and V. G. Kozlov. *Filosofskoye Naslediye V. I. Lenina i Problemy Sovremennoi Voiny (The Philosophical Heritage of V. I. Lenin and Problems of Contemporary War),* Voennoye Izdatel'stvo Ministerstva Oborony SSSR, Moscow, 1972.

"Olin, Nikolai." *"Govorit Radio 'Erevan'!"* ("Radio 'Erevan' Speaks!"), *Logos* (Munich, 1970).

———. *"Radio 'Erevan' Prodolzhayet Govorit' i Nachinayet Pokazyvat' "* ("Radio 'Erevan' Continues to Broadcast and Starts to Show"), *Bamizdat,* (1975).

Savkin, V. Ye. *Osnovniye Printsipy Operativnovo Iskusstva i Taktiki (The Basic Principles of Operational Art and Tactics),* Voennoye Izdatel'stvo Ministerstva Oborony SSSR, Moscow, 1972.

Sidorenko, Col. A. A. *Nastupleniye (Taking the Offensive),* Voennoye Izdatel'stvo, Ministerstva Oborony SSSR, Moscow, 1970.

Sokolovsky, V. D. *Soviet Military Strategy,* Crane, Russak & Company, Inc., New York, 1975. (Translated from the third Russian Edition, edited and annotated by Harriet Fast Scott.)

———. *Voennoye Strategiya (Military Strategy),* Voennoye Izdatel'stvo Ministerstva Oborony SSSR, 2d ed., Moscow, 1963.

———. *Voennoye Strategiya (Military Strategy),* Voennoye Izdatel'stvo Ministerstva Oborony SSSR, 1st ed., Moscow, 1962.

Stalin, J. V. *Sochineniya (Works),* Izdatel'stvo Politicheskoi Literatury, Moscow, 1952-1955, 13 vols.

Steinfeldt, Ye. *Chastotnii Slovar' Sovremennovo Russkovo Literaturnovo Yazyka (Frequency Dictionary of Contemporary Russian Literary Language),* Progress, Moscow, n.d.

Taylor, John W. R. (ed), *Jane's All the World's Aircraft 1975-76,* Franklin Watts, Inc., New York, 1975.

Index

181